Praise for *The Way*

"Maggie Oman Shannon has written a ter
book by gathering together many of the wo
practices and making them readily applicable to our own busy lives."

—CAROL ADRIENNE, PH.D., author of
Find Your Purpose, Change Your Life

"*The Way We Pray* is an exceptional and original resource guide to prayer practices from around the world from many different traditions. This book provides deep spiritual comfort, healing inspiration, and unlimited opportunities for daily renewal and active connection to life's mysteries. A major contribution to remembering the Divine within and without our natures!"

—ANGELES ARRIEN, PH.D., Cultural Anthropologist and
author of *The Four-Fold Way* and *Signs of Life*

"Maggie Oman Shannon has gifted us with a magnificent collage of practical grace. She has gathered together treasures from the family of the earth, precious jewels of prayer, contemplations and deep reflection. Any one of these offerings, if practiced, has the potential to bring us genuine peace and nourishment. To have so many wonderful stories and traditions at our disposal is a rich meal, indeed. Maggie's work is an astonishing act of love."

—WAYNE MULLER, author of
Sabbath and *How, Then, Shall We Live?*

Praise for *Prayers for Healing*

"I hope that people of all faiths as well as those who do not believe in a religion will find inspiration and understanding here that in some way contributes to their own inner peace."

—HIS HOLINESS THE DALAI LAMA

"An excellent resource for those who want to do more than just survive. Herein lies the wisdom of the ages."

—BERNIE SIEGEL, M.D., author of *Love, Medicine and Miracles*

THE WAY WE PRAY

Prayer Practices from Around the World

MAGGIE OMAN SHANNON

Foreword by ALAN JONES,
Dean of Grace Cathedral

CONARI PRESS
Berkeley, California

Conari Press books are distributed by Publishers Group West.

ISBN: 1-57324-571-2

Cover Photography: Jayanta Shaw REUTERS © Reuters NewMedia Inc./Corbis
Cover and Book Design: Suzanne Albertson

Library of Congress Cataloging-in-Publication Data

Oman Shannon, Maggie, 1958-
The way we pray : prayer practices from around the world / Maggie Oman Shannon.
p. cm.
Includes bibliographical references and index.
ISBN 1-57324-571-2
1. Prayer. I. Title.
BL560 .O63 2001
291.4'3—dc21 2001003038

Printed in Canada on recycled paper.

01 02 03 04 TR 10 9 8 7 6 5 4 3 2 1

This book is dedicated

to my husband,

Scott Bruce Shannon,

with deepest love, admiration, and gratitude

THE WAY WE PRAY

FOREWORD

Maggie Oman Shannon's book of prayer practices fills an important need for those of us who, ironically, have been brought up in a world of "know how" but have few skills for simply making ourselves available to the Divine. The danger, of course, is that we might turn our practice into the thing itself and become proficient in a sort of spiritual fussiness. But it would be foolish and sad for us to deprive ourselves of those practices and disciplines that ready us for the depths of joy and possibility promised us by such a relationship.

What we need to look for is an integrated spirituality: one that takes seriously the body, the mind, and the spirit. *The Way We Pray* offers us a treasury of integrating spiritual practices. Some of them may seem deceptively simple or even naïve. But the point to remember is that they all have the power to open us up to a deeper and more generous reality. The early theologians used to talk of God's economy. Because the Divine can never be fully known, we are given as much as we can bear as we go along. The Divine mystery comes to us in stages and in layers. As Gary Wills puts it, "To draw an angel with wings is an economy, meant to suggest some idea of a higher being to the young mind. It is false but not a lie." In other words, there is a spirit world far beyond our understanding, and it is personal and available to us. That's why, in the Divine economy, we talk of angels. This book is full of such wonderful instances of spiritual economy.

A friend of mine got frustrated recently when I attempted to explain to him the obligations of being a Christian: "I know there are a lot of things I am supposed to believe, but I am more interested in the question, 'What must I do?'" The exchange made me realize just how far some of us had drifted from the centrality of simple practice. There has always been something of a split in the great traditions between religion as gift and religion as task or response. The tendency in the West has been to ask, "What must I believe in order to be a Christian, a Jew, a Muslim, a Hindu, a Buddhist?" The other equally important question, "What must I do in order to be . . ." tends to get lost.

Our age suffers from over-rationalization, and we need to resist reductionist explanations of life's mysteries. No wonder our culture is depressed. The wonder and mystery tends to be sucked out of it. The solution is not to be uncritical or irrational, but to put the intellect in its proper place. One thing we need to affirm is that Spirit works through matter. I heard the following conversation not long ago about "near-death experiences." One person was talking about the sense of leaving the body, the sense of blissful well-being. The skeptic replied that all it was was oxygen deprivation: "The dying brain is starved of oxygen. This causes the neurons to rush about in an attempt to restore normalcy." The other person responded, "Why would such an 'explanation' invalidate the experience? We live in an age where descriptions masquerade as explanations. Of course, experiences have corresponding biochemical reactions. What would you expect? That's how God works." God works through our bodies, our minds, and our spirits, and what we do with them, how we "dispose" of them, makes a difference.

This wonderful handbook provides us with deep affirmations about the mystery of life. Such affirmations do not take away our pain and struggle, but they do place them in a larger and more generous vision of life that enables us to live in hope.

Finally, a word of gratitude. This book comes as an affirmation to me personally. For health reasons, I have chosen to take on a regime involving changes in diet and lifestyle. I practice yoga and other stress-reducing techniques every day. I exercise more regularly. These practices taken together have caused an inner spiritual revolution. I feel blessed that what I have believed all my life I am now, in a new way, beginning to practice. I believe this book will help others who are ready to put into practice what has long been waiting in their hearts. To help us on our journey, all we need to remember is the admonition of Saint John of the Cross, "In the end, we shall be examined in love." All our practice is in the service of love.

—Alan Jones,
Dean of Grace Cathedral
San Francisco

INTRODUCTION

Catherine of Siena wrote that "perfect prayer is achieved not with many words but with loving desire. . . . Everything you do can be a prayer"—and it is that thought, paired with a loving desire to contribute to a sense of the creative possibilities for prayer, that is at the heart of this book. In researching and writing *The Way We Pray,* my prayer has been to do justice to the practices described herein within a format that is inviting and accessible. I wished to honor not only these traditions but the people who have so graciously shared their stories about how they have made these practices, or elements of them, their own.

As is evident by the spectrum of practices described here, I am defining "prayer" broadly—and my motivation for doing so is the belief that by viewing prayer practice more expansively, our spiritual lives can be enriched. As cultural anthropologist Angeles Arrien reminds us, cross-culturally, "prayer" is a way of setting a sacred intention. Our early religious training may have drained the juice from how we set our sacred intentions; we may think of prayer as a daily requirement, as an emotional impulse that falls somewhere under the umbrella of the acronym ACTS—adoration, confession, thanksgiving, supplication—or even just as "talking to God." While these traditional outlooks may continue to quench the spiritual thirst of some practitioners throughout their lives, for others prayer often becomes rote and dry. By encouraging the exploration of what prayer can be, through the examination of practices used in different cultures throughout time, we may find new ways to encounter the Divine that will deepen both our experience and our understanding.

In an age where we have access to unprecedented amounts of current and historical information, there are new dialogues emerging regarding the appropriation of others' traditions. This can lead to a sort of spiritual fickleness. To continue this analogy, we are more able than ever before to pick and choose new partners to dance with or dine with (perhaps having little knowledge about their history or intentions), without committing to a single relationship. And sages in all major faith traditions have counseled that in order to truly immerse oneself in the spiritual life, one needs the discipline of a single path.

Wherever one sits in that debate, there is a distinction between religion and prayer. The purpose of *The Way We Pray* is not to encourage promiscuity of spiritual practice but to inspire a fidelity to the practice of prayer. By enlarging the arena in which we explore the Divine, we can expand our sense of the spiritual. In this way, prayer does not become something we do only at church or temple, or on bended knee at night, or when we're bargaining with God to get us a parking place or out of a tight spot. It becomes the enfolding fabric in which we live our lives, and everything we do has the potential to be prayerful.

Of course, the concept of prayer varies according to one's concept of God—whether you think God is outside of you or inside of you, or some indefinable combination of both. There's also the matter of the Christian Trinity and the pantheon of gods in the Hindu tradition, to name just two other theological considerations. In these belief systems, different entities—or aspects of God—are called upon in prayer for different purposes.

To address these fundamental differences, the definition of prayer I am working with here is not so much communicating with the Divine (although prayer can certainly incorporate that), but *communing* with the Divine—using prayer to place us in the presence of God. For some, this will suggest a relationship with God; for others, it will imply our spiritual identity as expressions of God.

Using the metaphor of prayer practices as soul food, think of this book as a menu posted in the window: giving enough of a description to tantalize you, sometimes including what others have said about their experience of the dish, but not the experience of a sit-down meal. That said, I hope my intention is clear—to provide a compendium of prayer practices with enough context to acknowledge the cultural traditions behind them, while offering an invitation for their further exploration. The suggestions given at the end of each chapter are inspired by the practices covered, and ask the reader how elements of them might call to be included in his or her existing prayer life. To return to the menu analogy, this book encourages you to consider new ingredients for prayer—and trusts that you will create your own meaningful recipe for putting them together. It is my hope that *The Way We Pray* will inspire and lead you to go within, to continue your own discoveries, to launch your own research, and to enjoy your own experience of each practice that beckons to you.

Enjoy is the operative word here, as it comes from the Latin word meaning "rejoice." We should approach prayer—and our God—joyfully; as Brother David Steindl-Rast reminds us in his book, *Gratefulness: The Heart of Prayer,* "It is never too late to recover that prayerfulness which is as natural to us as breathing. The child within us stays alive. And the child within us never loses the talent to look with the eyes of the heart, to combine concentration with wonderment, and so to pray without ceasing. The more we allow the child within us to come into its own, the more we become mature in our prayer life."

Finally, just as our concept of and relationship to the Sacred is as uniquely individual as we are, so will our prayer life be. Whether you choose one prayer practice or use many, the form always follows function; and the function of prayer is to transcend one's worldly experience and dwell in the Holy. When choosing the means of doing so, it is helpful—no matter what faith path you follow—to remember the words found in the New Testament's 1 Thessalonians 5:21: "Test everything. Hold on to the good."

AFFIRMATIONS

Employing God's Gifts

The soul is dyed the color of its thoughts.
Think only on those things that are in line with your principles and can bear the full light of day. The content of your character is your choice. Day by day, what you choose, what you think, and what you do is who you become. . . .

—HERACLITUS

Like a number of disciplines that have become diluted, even muddied, through the popularity of their practice, the word *affirmations* can either raise eyebrows or elicit enthusiastic examples of their efficacy. Some stories about affirmations have become part of our modern folklore: the $10 million check for "acting services rendered" that Jim Carrey wrote to himself just years before he made the news for being signed for that exact amount; the discipline of writing daily, "I will become a syndicated cartoonist," by *Dilbert* creator Scott Adams—with the result that he not only became a syndicated cartoonist but, thanks to enthusiastic merchandising efforts, a millionaire as well.

Affirmations as we know them were brought to the public eye in the nineteenth century through the work of French pharmacist Dr. Emile Coué. In the 1870s, Coué became fascinated by the power of the mind, practicing "mind conditioning therapy" in his free clinic. One of the first and best-known phrases defined as an affirmation comes from Coué: "Every day in every way I'm getting better and better." As that example illustrates, effective affirmations follow similar guidelines: they are focused on a specific goal (such as cartoonist Adams'); they use the present tense ("I love and accept myself"); they are positive and focus on the desired outcome ("I feel wonderful and radiate perfect health"); they are short and easily memorized; and they are repeated out loud or written down several times a day for weeks—often longer.

While affirmations are a proven psychological tool for enhancing success—they are used in combination with visualization by top performers in every field, including business, sports, and entertainment—they do have roots in older, more spiritual arenas. Indeed, as authors Willis Harman and Howard Rheingold wrote in *Higher Creativity,* "In institutionalized religions, prayer probably originated as a living exercise in affirmation, but degenerated to a ritual of supplication or penance directed toward some external being. Yet those whose devotion leads them to the true meaning beneath the outer form of their religion's prayers come to realize that it is not an external message system, but a dialogue between self and Self, a channel to the wisest of our inner personalities."

According to spiritual teacher Paramahansa Yogananda,

who nearly fifty years ago wrote a book on affirmations titled *Scientific Healing Affirmations,*

> The Lord helps those who help themselves. He gave you will power, concentration, faith, reason, and common sense to use when trying to rid yourself of bodily and mental afflictions; you should employ all those powers while simultaneously appealing to Him.
>
> As you utter prayers or affirmations, always believe that you are using *your own* but *God-given* powers to heal yourself or others. Ask His aid; but realize that you yourself, as His beloved child, are employing His gifts of will, emotion, and reason to solve all difficult problems of life. A balance should be struck between the medieval idea of wholly depending on God and the modern way of sole reliance on the ego.

Affirmations, used as a prayer practice, help us to focus on the Divine and to affirm ourselves as spiritual beings with creative power. Using the "I am" format of affirmations echoes the name of God: "I AM THAT I AM." Being mindful of what follows the "I am" construction is crucial, because there is great power in that declarative sentence. It is wise to use it to affirm that which you want enhanced in your life, not to announce that with which you are dissatisfied.

Shakti Gawain, author of *Creative Visualization,* and Louise Hay, author of various books, including *You Can Heal Your Life,* are two contemporary writers who have helped to bring the practice of affirmations into popular, even mainstream, use. Hay also created a compendium of healing affirmations to treat specific illnesses, believing—as a survivor of cancer—that what we say to ourselves does have the power to positively affect our health. Writes Hay, "We have learned that for every effect in our lives, there is a thought pattern that precedes and maintains it. Our consistent thinking patterns create our experiences. Therefore, by changing our thinking patterns, we can change our experiences."

New Age wishful thinking? Not when you place it in the context of New Testament scripture, which, in Philippians 4:8, advises us that "whatever is true, whatever is noble, whatever is right, whatever is pure, whatever is lovely, whatever is admirable—if anything is excellent or praiseworthy—think about such things." Here, it would seem, we're asked to affirm that "I am a unique and valuable expression of God," not to whine "I am so fat." Though we're all familiar with the nursery rhyme that proclaims, "Words will never hurt me," practitioners of affirmations believe that words can hurt us if we repeat them often enough—especially if we believe that they're true. Jesus, in Matthew 21:22, indicates why we should watch our words so carefully: "If you believe, you will receive whatever you ask for in prayer."

Suggestions for Beginning the Exploration

- Choose an area of your life that you feel has been an impediment to your spiritual life—such as feeling you don't have the time to go to church or temple or to volunteer for a cause you believe in; spending too much time watching television instead of reading uplifting material; or not scheduling a consistent period of prayer and meditation. Create affirmations that will support you in these endeavors—for instance, "I enjoy my schedule, which allows me the time to engage in activities that nourish my soul" or, "As I turn off the television channels, channels for good and channels for God open up in my life."

- Surround yourself with your affirmations—put them on mirrors, in your day planner, on your car dashboard, on your computer at work.
- Begin an affirmation journal, and keep a record of the changes you see manifesting in your life.

ALTARS

A Place to Grow Your Soul

Through an altar, including the objects placed on it and the acts performed around it, a person invokes and has a relationship with the transcendent. It's a place to invite, to talk to, and to know God. It's a place of aspiration of and dedication to ideals. It's a place to bring and grow your soul.

—EDWARD SEARL

Altars are as ancient as civilization itself, and, paralleling our own social, psychological, and theological development, the use of altars has evolved as we humans have. The word *altar* derives from the Latin *adolere,* meaning "to burn up." Indeed, as the dictionary further reminds us, the classic definition of altar is "a usually raised structure or place on which sacrifices are offered or incense is burned in worship." Altars historically have been used in exactly that order in earlier societies, for dark and fear-based rites sometimes involving live sacrifices, and later, as a platform for holy accoutrements specific to the religion being practiced (and usually accessible only to those who were proclaimed the intermediaries to the Divine). Today, altars are undergoing a renaissance in Western society and are being used in creative, new ways that are both empowering and deeply individualistic.

The practice of creating a personal altar is one that we do naturally, instinctively. Whether or not they view it as an altar, most people have groupings of personally significant elements in their homes, such as framed photographs of loved ones, special candles or fresh flowers in a beautiful vase, and cherished treasures from a dear friend or family member. The only thing that would distinguish these arrangements from what many are calling their personal altars is simply the conscious intention behind them.

In both this kind of tableau and on a personal altar, the objects chosen for placement are visual reminders of what's most beautiful, true, and precious in our lives. What transforms a tabletop arrangement into an altar is the intention to make that space sacred, to use it as a place where we can acknowledge the God of our understanding. The altar then becomes a sensory cue to transform the way we are holding ourselves, our lives, our hopes and fears; in front of our personal altars, we indeed sacrifice or surrender our lower thought forms as we shift our consciousness to honor a Higher Power.

Eleanor Wiley is a former speech therapist who currently makes and leads workshops on contemporary prayer beads all over the world. Eleanor's funky Victorian house and studio are full of altars and small corner shrines; it is a prayer practice she's engaged in since she was seven. Explains

Eleanor, "My altars are ways of reminding me that our whole lives are sacred. My first visit to Bali made it a more conscious thing, because the Balinese honor every facet of their lives; they don't exclude anything.

"It is important to have representations of all faith paths around me, and on my primary altar—which includes pictures of my family, Nelson Mandela, a monk I met in Thailand, and the Dalai Lama; a dressed Ganesh doll from India; a cross from El Salvador; and a brass fish figurine that is inscribed with the words 'Celebrate Life'—I keep reminders of both the wonderful and the awful things that have happened in my life. A lot of the objects on that altar remind me that we only have today.

"I think what's really important to say about altars is that people don't have to go out and get something special for them—it can be anything. It's about keeping your space sacred rather than thinking it has to look a certain way. The reason I have so many altars is to keep them in my consciousness—so that when I see them, I'll come into the present moment and say a prayer."

In addition to including elements that remind one of inspirational figures or beloved friends, family members, or pets, items placed on a personal altar can have symbolic significance. In her book *Altars Made Easy,* author Peg Streep delineates a number of approaches one can use mindfully when creating a personal altar. For example, deliberately placing an altar in a particular direction can be significant to one's spiritual focus, as can the lore and symbology behind different numbers, colors, animal representations, stones, flowers, plants, and herbs.

In addition, altars can be created for specific intentions. When entering the doors of Asian-owned businesses, one often sees small raised altars replete with incense and offerings such as flowers and mandarin oranges. During Mexico's Day of the Dead festival, ancestors who are no longer living are commemorated with elaborate *ofrendas,* which include candles, marigolds, religious icons, and the ancestor's favorite foods and drink, along with sweet breads in the shape of people and sugar skulls.

As Denise Linn suggests in *Altars: Bringing Sacred Shrines into Your Everyday Life,* possibilities for altars are as far ranging as the concerns in a human life. One can make altars for love, abundance, fertility, creativity; for new relationships, new marriage, or a new baby; for remembering one who has died or for mourning the completion of a relationship; for celebrating and setting intentions for a birthday, anniversary, vacation, or new project. One can also use the same altar to hold the various intentions and focuses of one's life. No matter what our approach or our practices, we all touch common—and holy—ground when we create a personal altar. In the words of writer-photographer Jean McMann, who has been making altars since she was eight or nine, "Arranging and celebrating them, we give shape to our world, visible and invisible."

Suggestions for Beginning the Exploration

- Take a look around your living space. Note the arrangements you have in place already. Do any of them represent your sense of the Mystery? You may have an altar in place without consciously acknowledging it as such.

- If not, mindfully gather items that will support your prayer life. These could include a candle, a book of sacred scripture or poetry, or fresh flowers. Return to this place to pray and meditate, and, if you feel called to do so, add to your altar collection.

AMULETS

Reminders of the Most Sacred

The entire journey in God is a journey in symbols. . . .

—LALECH BAKHTIAR

Picture these: a pewter angel, a copper medal depicting the Hindu elephant god Ganesh, a blue glass anti-evil eye charm, a clay scarab, a rose-quartz pendant, a walnut carved with 108 likenesses of Buddha. Though the wearing or carrying of amulets may seem to be a material flourish of this generation's New Age movement, the practice is as old as human history itself. Every culture and every major world religion has a particular way of enfolding amulets into its spiritual practice, though there are differing interpretations on why or when to use them. Though we're not always aware of it, we use amulets throughout our lives, ascribing sentimental or symbolic significance to inanimate objects: a wedding ring that reminds the wearer of loving vows made to another, or a "lucky" pen given at graduation with blessings for future success.

The Roman naturalist Pliny first described differing types of amulets, drawing a distinction between those that offered ameliorative or healing effects to the wearer and those that served a protective function. As George Frederick Kunz wrote in his 1915 work, *The Magic of Jewels and Charms,* "It is sometimes difficult to establish a hard and fast dividing line between the two classes, as everything that conduces to the happiness and well-being of man also affects his bodily health." Others have used the term *talisman* to refer to a charm that wards off negative influences and *amulet* for a charm that serves as a magnet for good—though, interestingly, the word *amulet* is derived from the Latin *amuletum* or *amoletum,* meaning "means of defense."

Using amulets can become a prayer practice when the object connotes a communication to the Divine or is carried as a reminder of that which is most sacred to the wearer—although it could be argued that any intention behind the amulet is itself a prayer. The ancient Egyptians were great employers of amulets, many of which depicted Egyptian deities; ancient pagans also wore figurines of their gods. Pieces of paper holding quotations from sacred religious texts—including the Torah, New Testament, and Koran—have been carried in containers that served as amulets; today, mezuzahs containing inscribed verses from the Old Testament are fixed near the door of Jewish homes as a sign and reminder of their faith. The carved fetishes of indigenous cultures pay homage to the sacred qualities embodied by the subject; tiny Buddhist prayer stones represent a range of spiritual figures. Islamic amulets are carved in calligraphy with scriptural verses or a list of the attributes of God; medals depicting various patron saints are worn by Catholics for comfort. The contemporary

"WWJD" jewelry—and the subsequent "WWBD" rejoinders—reminds the wearer to ask, "What would Jesus (or Buddha) do?" in challenging circumstances.

For Celeste Smeland, an artist and nonprofit arts administrator, wearing an amulet has brought forth spiritual fruit for a decade. For more than ten years, she has worn a pendant of watermelon tourmaline—it derives its name from its gradation of color from green to red—around her neck. For her, it is a reminder and a prayer to keep her heart open.

Celeste shares her story: "In 1990, my longtime partner/husband/soulmate and I were feeling the beginnings of the end of our relationship. At the same time this was happening, a number of my friends had died or were dying from AIDS. Additionally, a few of my female friends were suffering from cancer—one died. So it was a time of heartfelt loss.

"There was this little shop close to our house—kind of a 'New Age' place—with crystals, tarot cards, and books. I went in there often, as I found it a welcoming place of repose.

"So, as I could feel the crumbling of our relationship and our partnership was growing ever more difficult, I found myself drawn to this little watermelon tourmaline at this shop. I would come back and visit it often before I finally decided to buy it. I simply felt compelled.

"After I bought it and put it on and it dropped down around my neck and came to rest just above my heart, I felt a warmth and a heart opening. I asked the woman who owned the shop what it was and if it had a 'purpose.' She told me it was a watermelon tourmaline and that it was a 'heart opener.'

"Well, you can imagine my surprise. But, I must say it felt like my guardian angel as I went through all the changes and pains of that breakup. Whenever the pain got really tough, I would hold the crystal in my hands or roll it around in my fingers, and it always made me feel better—helped to center me. And yet, I am pleased to say, even though I have worn it nearly every day since, it has never felt superstitious or intense—just soft, gentle, warm—and a trigger for helping to open my heart to the possibilities of life and personal connection."

Taoists in China use amulets for general healing and protection; while users of amulets in Japan often have more specific intentions for them, such as scholastic success or safety while driving. Whatever your prayer, you might discover—as Celeste did—that wearing or carrying an amulet opens your heart to a world of possibilities.

Suggestions for Beginning the Exploration

- Look around your living space. Do you notice anything that you already consider to be an amulet? Are you drawn to collecting hearts or sun-catchers or bowls? Do you have a piece of jewelry you always wear? Spend some time with your journal in investigating what spiritual significance these may have for you.
- If you don't have anything that represents your spiritual life, pay attention to what you're drawn to—what makes your heart (or soul) sing. Is it roses or sunflowers? Are there images in your spiritual readings that compel you?

Try looking for a small representation of that image and wear it or carry it with you. Notice if having something you can look at and touch helps you to pray more often.

ANGELS

Messengers from God

Angels can give wings to our prayers,
they carry our prayers to God, to the infinite
realm where all things are possible.

—TERRY LYNN TAYLOR

Modern-day mention of angels ranges from the sublime to the ridiculous, as angels appear not only in the ancient scriptures of major religions but also in our contemporary pop culture. From songs ("Earth Angel") to television shows *(Touched by an Angel)*, from magazines *(Angels on Earth)* to films *(Wings of Desire)*, angels not only are being entertained, they have become entertainment.

Though the blending of the popular and the spiritual may have created some confusion as to what angels are and how they fit into a prayer practice, there is general agreement that they are instruments of God; the word *angel* comes from the Greek word *aggelos*, meaning "messenger." Angels are found in the Islamic, Jewish, and Christian traditions, classified into hierarchies, and are seen, as their name would imply, as bearers of Divine revelation. In most cultures, they are viewed as benevolent, looking after us as our "guardian angels" and sometimes intervening where we need a helping hand. How much of a role do they play? Theologians have been discussing this, and other needling points, for centuries; the Indian poet Rabindranath Tagore had this to say: "I believe we are free, within limits, and yet there is an unseen hand, a guiding angel, that somehow, like a submerged propeller, drives us on."

Kathy Kidd, a customer service supervisor for a major automotive company, has firsthand knowledge of how a guiding angel can drive one on. Working with angels has become a deeply important prayer practice for Kathy since she was diagnosed with cancer at the age of forty-four. She explains:

"Having been diagnosed with Stage IIIA breast cancer and consequently undergoing a bilateral mastectomy, I unexpectedly received the gift of prayer. I had been diagnosed a year earlier, but was told the cancer cells were formed and confined to the ducts. At that time, I decided I had three choices: do nothing; have a mastectomy, radiation, and possibly chemotherapy; or seek alternative treatment. I chose the latter because in my mind I had time to reverse this process, since it had been caught in the early stages. I later found out I was probably misdiagnosed and that the cancer cells were further along in the process than originally diagnosed.

"I began a variety of alternative treatments, and in the process began to more deeply explore my spiritual nature. This was not new to me, except that now I was desperate, and open to anything and everything. I took a workshop on guardian angels. During that experience I was able to visualize my guardian angel and experience her energy—it was so sweet, and it filled me with waves of love and acceptance. In one of the exercises, we practiced sending the energy of our angel to each other. It was my first experience of consciously sending energy to another person and having them tell me how that energy felt. My partner felt my angel's sweetness and feminine energy in waves also—even though we had not yet shared our own experiences of how our angels' energy felt. I felt my partner's angel energy as masculine and pulsating. She confirmed that that was indeed her same energy experience. I have since realized that we give and receive energy continually and constantly. We are pure energy.

"Prior to this, I was consciously aware that every thought and belief is heard by God and is a prayer. I had become very careful about my thoughts. I deduced that since we are pure energy, then thoughts have energy. That energy is either negative or positive, depending on your thoughts—which are prayers. We are a living, breathing prayer every moment of our life. I also had this belief validated in another way that was more experiential than logical.

"In my experience with cancer, I have had people do things for me and I have chosen to give back to them through prayer. Initially, it was out of helplessness. I was physically unable to do anything except pray. When I realized the beauty of the energy I was giving, I began to tune in to energy and I had a deep knowing that life is a living, breathing prayer. When I send energy to others—pray—I know that people are also receiving my angel's sweet hypnotic energy. She and my soul are one. Sometimes I will ask to feel her energy, and a sweet wave of love will infuse me. Whenever I pray, I talk to her and God together.

"I began to pray without needing an immediate answer. I discovered that if I turn over questions to God and my angels, I create an open space for the answers to come in their own time. A cluttered soul that has forgotten to clean, clear, and simplify through prayer must default to the personality, which makes decisions that may not be the best path.

"Each morning and evening, as part of my prayer practices, I thank my guardian angel and God for their guidance. I also ask God to reveal to my angel any information needed to assist me on my path. I pray for direction in opening myself to her guidance, and I pray that my personality will take a backseat to her wisdom.

"Before or after meditation, I call upon her presence, her energy. I pray to her like I pray to God. In fact, at this point, I cannot pray to one without including the other. I realized how inseparable they are—indeed, how inseparable we all are."

As Kathy's account so dramatically illustrates, experiencing an angel's presence is transformative. Given the important role that angels play in most world religions, it might make sense to follow the suggestion of Saint Francis de Sales: "Make yourself familiar with the angels, and behold them frequently in spirit. Without being seen, they are present with you."

Suggestions for Beginning the Exploration

- Start noticing angel imagery or written references to

angels as you go about your day-to-day routine, or go to a store that specializes in angel gifts and books. How do you feel as you contemplate, or let yourself be immersed in, these representations?

- Read accounts of those who have been visited or "touched" by angels. Does reading about others' experiences inspire you to sift back through yours? Have you ever entertained an angel, unaware?
- If you do not currently believe that you have a guardian angel, imagine that you did. How would that affect your everyday life? How would it affect your spiritual life? If you are drawn to investigate this possibility further, do an Internet search on angels and study some of the many books that have been written about angels (some suggestions are in the "For Further Reading" section at the back of this book).

Body Prayer

Worship in the Temple of God

The body is the sacred sanctuary of the soul.

—Ilana Rubenfeld

In Aramaic, the definition of the word *prayer* is opening ourselves so that the Divine can fill our lives, both inside and out. Using our bodies as a tool for that opening has been practiced in different forms, by different cultures, for thousands of years.

One of the best-known forms of body prayer—yoga—is an Indian discipline of self-realization that has been practiced for 4,000 years and is enjoying new popularity in the Western world. From the word meaning "to unite," "yoke," or "join together," yoga uses a combination of meditation, breath control, and physical postures to reconnect with God. The postures, called *asanas,* embody this intention. And while modern devotees of yoga speak about the physical and emotional benefits of this practice, they make a distinction between using it as a trendy form of exercise and using it as a spiritual path. But the challenges that are inherent in yoga's demands will bring forth new understandings, even if one's purpose for studying yoga isn't primarily spiritual; encountering the body's resistance to a difficult move also requires facing one's mind and heart.

Mudras, the positioning of the hands and fingers into particular postures during meditation, are another form of body prayer that comes out of the Hindu tradition. It is believed that mudras not only can bring forth a different state of consciousness, but also invoke the presence of particular deities. Hand movements, too, are emphasized in other religions; in the New Testament, we are asked to "lift up holy hands in prayer" (1 Timothy 2:8). Throughout time, people have employed body movements in prayer; the Romans used to stand with arms raised, and early Christians would pray with their arms extended to acknowledge Christ on the cross. Today, worshipers on various faith paths raise their hands or eyes toward heaven, bow their heads, kneel, genuflect, make a sign of the cross, and prostrate themselves in prayer. For some of them, the act of taking off their shoes signifies their walk on holy ground, or serves as a way to "ground" them.

If the body is the temple of God and God's Spirit lives in us, as 1 Corinthians 3:16 tells us, then it seems a natural extension to employ the body while worshiping God. But for many people, "Let us pray" is simply an invitation to bow our heads, ignoring the other possibilities for embodied prayer that are always ours. Some people, in reaction to harsh religious teachings that have emphasized the unworthiness of the worshiper, refuse to bow their heads, feeling that doing so disavows the concept of God's Spirit as an intrinsic part of us.

Body prayer integrates the experience of prayer on the

physical, mental, and spiritual levels. And because it does, there are new approaches being developed all the time. One practice is even called BodyPrayer, which, according to its promotional materials, is "a form of systemic, or whole-being movement, which draws on the wisdom and practice of many traditions, Eastern and Western, modern and ancient... [making] it possible to feed the Body-Mind-Spirit with a whole variety of movement food." Similar to this is Celtic Body Prayers, "a new approach to balancing body with gentle exercise, mind with meditation, and spirit with prayer." Dancer Gabrielle Roth's "The Wave"—which takes practitioners through five cadences: flowing, staccato, chaos, lyrical, and stillness—is a powerful symbol of life itself.

Whether you choose to follow an established form of body prayer or experiment with new approaches, it is important to make your movements meaningful to you. As the following story demonstrates, the power of body prayer lies in its personal significance.

Bruce Zuckerman is a self-employed personal clothier and marathon runner. His experience with body prayer began when he joined a support group for alcoholism in the late '80s, and his sponsor advised him to get down on his knees every morning and say a prayer. Before that, Bruce's prayer life was nonexistent: "I associated prayer with religion, and I had rejected my religion." But his sponsor's insistence that Bruce literally get on his knees every morning launched a practice that now is deeply important to him.

"For me, it began very rote—like, I've *got* to do this. I didn't embrace the prayer concept very readily; for the first three years in, I simply read the prayers. But after a while, I found that I would start saying other things—talking. It became a ritual: In the morning, I get on my knees and ask for help; in the evening, I get on my knees and say thank you. Also in the morning I read two spiritual books and reflect on the message. I try to clear my head and be quiet—and that could be anywhere from one minute to twenty. I also take those thoughts with me into exercise—it's all part of doing what I need to do to be present for the day. When I'm running, I can virtually guarantee that sometime during that period, I'm going to be talking to God.

"Every day, at the very least, I'm on my knees to connect. When I've overslept and don't have time, I'll do it later—I've even knelt in the latrine and by a Dumpster! I do that out of a belief that it's part of my discipline—it's a pact. I have to do that certain basic minimum: which is to get on my knees, asking for help, acknowledging that there's something out there. I have to embody it in some kind of action."

Whatever form of action you choose to embody in your prayer life, staying mindful of your body as a dwelling for the Divine will enhance your spiritual experience. Attendant with that is the need to treat our bodies well; as spiritual teacher Nisargadatta taught, "Do not neglect this body. This is the house of God; take care of it. Only in this body can God be realized."

Suggestions for Beginning the Exploration

- Begin to experiment with simple body movements as you pray—perhaps, at first, just using your arms and hands. As you move them to represent gratitude, joy, humility, awe, what changes do you note internally? Track your experiences as you begin to embody prayer.
- Try a yoga class or a dance class based on Gabrielle Roth's work. Notice how incorporating movement into your prayer life moves you emotionally and spiritually.

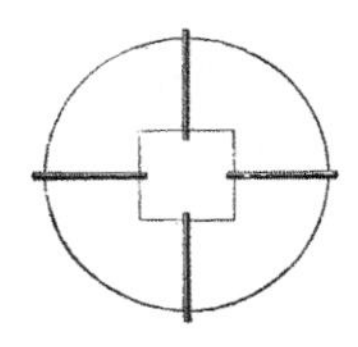

Centering Prayer

Opening Our Whole Being

The root of prayer is interior silence. We may think of prayer as thoughts or feelings expressed in words, but this is only one expression. Deep prayer is the laying aside of thoughts. It is the opening of mind and heart, body, and feelings—our whole being—to God, the Ultimate Mystery, beyond word, thoughts, and emotions.

—Thomas Keating

The adage "What's old is new again" is certainly appropriate when referring to Centering Prayer, a form of contemplative prayer that was drawn from the ancient prayer practices of the Desert Fathers and Mothers. In addition to the Desert Fathers and Mothers, practitioners included the anonymous fourteenth-century author of *The Cloud of Unknowing*, Saint Teresa of Avila, Saint John of the Cross, and many others. The practice was reintroduced in the 1970s by three Trappist monks at St. Joseph's Abbey in Spencer, Massachusetts—Father William Meninger, Father Basil Pennington, and Abbot Thomas Keating.

Although this form of prayer was seen as the goal of spirituality for the first sixteen centuries of the church, the tradition was effectively lost after the Reformation. Largely due to the efforts of the three men mentioned, Centering Prayer is entering a stage of fervent renewal. Perhaps part of the reason for this is the inherent healing function of Centering Prayer. As Thomas Keating said in a 1998 interview in *Spirituality and Health* magazine, "One of the great advantages of Centering Prayer is that it's like taking a vacation from the false self for twenty minutes twice a day. . . . Contemplative prayer is really the healing of body, mind, and spirit."

Centering Prayer is the method used for, or the process of, contemplative prayer in the Christian tradition, although people of all faith paths can use this form. As the sixth-century Gregory the Great expressed it, its focus is resting in God, being in communion with the Divine in an attitude of silence. It has some similarities to Eastern meditation in that it involves the use of a single word, repeated like a mantra: possibilities include "Jesus," "peace," "shalom," "love," "Abba." (Because of this, some have referred to Centering Prayer as *monologion*, or one-word prayer.) Like a mantra, the repetition of the word serves as a focal point, a marker to return to when distracted by other thoughts.

Centering Prayer begins with the intention to be with God; practitioners of Centering Prayer advocate doing it twice a day, in sessions of approximately twenty minutes each. The format is simple: Choose your sacred word, position yourself comfortably, repeat the word when your thoughts intrude during this time of prayer, then conclude the session gradually and gently. Though one might feel he or she has received insights or new understandings around the sacred word chosen, that is not the point of Centering Prayer—and in fact, practitioners are encouraged to simply return to the word rather than follow the train of thought. Thought is seen as an impediment to the experience of God, which is the reward of contemplative prayer. As the author of *The Cloud of Unknowing* wrote, "If you strive to fix your love on him forgetting all else, which is the work of contemplation I have urged you to begin, I am confident that God in his goodness will bring you to a deep experience of himself."

From these roots in the Middle Ages, Centering Prayer has joined the age of the Internet; *www.centeringprayer.com* is one of several Web sites devoted to information about the practice. After defining what it is not, the Web site authors then provide their definition of Centering Prayer: "It is at the same time a relationship with God and a discipline to foster relationship; it is an exercise of faith, hope, and love; it is a movement beyond conversation with Christ to communion; it habituates us to the language of God, which is silence."

Suggestions for Beginning the Exploration

- Take a word that has meaning for you, such as *love,* and carry it with you into prayer and meditation. Hold the word tenderly; this is not a time for analysis or cognition. When you are distracted by thoughts of other things, gently return to the word you've chosen.
- After you have spent time in prayer, consider: Did holding this word in prayer deepen your experience of prayer?

CEREMONIAL COSTUMES

Adorning the Silence and the Singing

Worship the Lord in the beauty of holiness.

—1 CHRONICLES 16:29

From the dawn of civilization, art and worship have been inextricably intertwined. Most obviously, they are companions in the form of ceremonial costumes, special headdresses or masks, or clothing or jewelry that is worn to transcend the everyday world and shimmer as invitingly as the transcendent.

From the elaborately crafted clothing that ancient Egyptians, Chinese, and pre-Columbian peoples used to bury their dead and to bless their experience in the afterlife to the modern vestments of the Christian church, which symbolize promises of Scripture (for instance, a special liturgical belt is worn by bishops and priests while they recite psalms to remind them that it is God who "girds them with strength"), ceremonial costumes have been a universal form of acknowledging the Divine.

These adornments range from the primitive to the fine, and sometimes evolved from one extreme to another. For instance, the Japanese Buddhist priests' robe, called a *kesa,* originally was made from old pieces of cloth, even rags, in obedience to their vows of poverty. With time, as Buddhist ceremony became more elaborate, so, too, did the *kesa.* In nearby China, clothing—like its art—has historically been adorned with sacred symbols, such as the endless knot, a symbol of Buddha, or waves, which symbolize the cosmos.

In Africa, the wearing of *kente* cloth was originally reserved for sacred occasions, used in ceremonies including child naming, marriage, and soul washing. There are more than 300 different types of *kente*-cloth design, each with a special name and meaning. Colors have particular significance; for example, blue represents the Supreme Creator, as it is the color of the sky and thus symbolizes spirituality, peacefulness, and love. Black symbolizes spiritual maturity; thus ritual objects are sometimes blackened to increase their power.

Masks have a history dating back to the ancient Greeks; the use of masks is found on virtually every continent. Cultures in South America, Australia, Africa, Asia, Europe, and North America all have used masks in sacred ceremonies. In the United States, the Pueblo Indians' masked and costumed dancers represent *kachina,* deified ancestral spirits. In Mexico, during the Day of the Dead festival held annually at the beginning of November, people celebrate with masks in the shape of skulls.

Why are human beings drawn to costume or ceremonial clothing as a form of worship? Perhaps because it is a means of tangibly breaking out of everyday routine to mark, through texture and color, an entrance into sacred space.

As Lynn Baskfield's story shows, what makes a ceremonial costume sacred is the meaning that it provides to the individual. Lynn is a storyteller, seminar leader, and personal coach. A lover of beauty, Lynn was entranced by a pair of shoes she saw in a catalog that were pink, blue, purple, and yellow, adorned with moons, stars, and gold spirals across the toes. Says Lynn, "To me they were magic shoes and I wanted a pair, but they didn't come in my size: 11. I began lusting over those magic shoes, thinking that I could make some myself if I just had time. There was something about the shoes that was so attractive—I knew I needed them to express a part of me."

At the time, Lynn was not only finishing a master's degree but a book, as well as designing workshops that would be held in another country. She could not see any time in her schedule for making magic shoes—but she did decide to at least find out what kind of shoe dye she could use when she finally did get around to making them. Shopping for that shoe dye started her on a roll—and soon the jars of colored shoe dye and black and gold acrylic paint landed on her newspaper-covered dining room table.

Lynn remembers, "I felt alive again in a way that the schoolwork and deadlines, though stimulating, didn't provide. I looked at those shoes from all different angles—my whole body was engaged. Touch, smell, sight, movement, voice—a creative dance had begun and I couldn't stop. They are the most fun, beautiful pair of shoes I could ever imagine. I tie them with turquoise laces.

"I realized as I was creating those shoes that I was creating the magic. I can dance in my magic shoes. I can sing. I am grounded in my life. Standing squarely in the center of my life, at the still point in the ever-revolving wheel, in my magic shoes I hear the silence and the singing."

Lynn has gone on to teach other people how to make them in her workshops, ending with a ritual in which everyone puts on their magic shoes and walks forward together. Says Lynn, "People do different things with their shoes; they use beads, feathers, sequins. That serves to symbolize our different purposes. The shoes reflect how we walk forth into life—how we walk our purpose."

It is the creative aspect of making ceremonial costumes that Lynn sees as a prayer practice, citing author Julia Cameron's phrase that "creativity is to the soul what blood is to the body." Lynn elaborates, "I don't think it matters so much what you create, as *that* you create. It doesn't have to be shoes; it could be robes, scarves, button covers. The point is to be bold and tell your creative truth: that's the prayer. It brings me very close to Spirit to say 'Yes' to the creative self.

"It's an ongoing unfoldment, and it lightens up prayer practice—women in my workshops have joked about walking up to receive communion in their magic shoes. It just gives another whole dimension to what prayer is and can be."

By creating ceremonial costumes, these visual ways to shift our consciousness from the everyday to the sacred, we honor the Mystery. We become creators ourselves, working with the palette of the beautiful. It is a powerful force, as British theologian William Ralph Inge reminds us: "The love of beauty is super-personal and disinterested, like all the spiritual values; it promotes common enjoyment and social sympathy. Unquestionably it is one of the three ultimate values, ranking with Goodness and Truth."

Suggestions for Beginning the Exploration

- Is there something you already own that suggests sacred ceremony to you? If not, consider making something, as Lynn did. A jacket, hat, mask, stole, scarf, or vest are all items that you could create or adapt for marking your sacred time.
- Try entering your prayer time with your ceremonial clothing on, and without it. Does wearing your ceremonial clothing enhance your spiritual experience?

CHANTS

Raising Our Voices to God

God hears no sweeter music than the cracked chimes of the courageous human spirit ringing in imperfect acknowledgment of His perfect love.

—JOSHUA LOTH LIEBMAN

Imagine hearing a sweet, flutelike, feminine soprano on one side of you and a deep, resonant masculine bass on the other, as you feel the notes of your own voice combine with your companions' voices to vibrate inside you. This vibration is not only deeply soothing, it can actually alter your consciousness—some say it can connect you with the Divine. This vibration is the heart of chanting.

The practice of chanting is found in all of the major religious traditions. Chants are also spiritually significant to many cultures, including the Native American and Hawaiian. Ranging from melodic Christian chants to the single notes of Tibetan Buddhist monks, rhythmic African chants to liturgical Jewish chants, it offers a large spectrum of musical possibility. Because of this range, perhaps the best definition of chant is the one that musician and author Robert Gass gives in his book *Chanting:* "Chant is singing our prayers. Chant is vocal meditation. Chant is the breath made audible in tone. Chant is 'discovering Spirit in sound.'"

Humankind has been chanting since the dawn of civilization. For thousands of years, both Hindus and Buddhists have chanted the word *om;* not only is the word a sacred syllable, but the effects of chanting it have symbolic consequence. As Layne Redmond writes in *When the Drummers Were Women: A Spiritual History of Rhythm,* "The sacred mantra OM is considered the seed syllable of created existence. If intoned correctly, it vibrates the cranium and the cerebral cortex of the brain, causing a sound similar to the humming of bees. This mantra and its sound are linked to the omphalos, the great beehive—the place of sacred utterance and the buzzing vibration of life."

Chanting has been practiced in the Jewish tradition for at least 3,000 years; liturgical chant was a means to proclaim the sacred scriptures to those in the congregation. The Christian church inherited the custom of chanting from its Jewish origins and developed several distinct schools of chant, including the rediscovered Gregorian chants, which rode a wave of popularity in the mid-1990s, when the recordings of the Benedictine monks of Santo Domingo de Silos topped music charts.

Attaching song to sacred texts allows an emotive quality that the mere speaking of it cannot; it allows us to move beyond our usual rational, left-brain consciousness into another plane of perception. And because it affects our physiology through its vibration, it can have highly healing effects—indeed, some healers intuitively use sounds, or toning, directed at the wounded or constricted parts of another's body.

Chanting is also viewed as a form of mantra yoga, seen as extending beyond a simple act of praying into a specific spiritual discipline, because it incorporates breath control and particular postures. As such, it is believed to be transformative both for body and soul. Other traditions acknowledge chant's ameliorative effects; as one Sikh chant implores, "From ignorance, to Reality, lead me; From dullness, to Illumination, lead me; From being mortal, to Immortality."

Whether one practices a formal system of chanting or decides to experiment with intoning a spiritual word or phrase to enhance existing prayer practices, the vibrations that reverberate internally and externally will strum one's sense of the Sacred. As the Talmud (Tikkune Zohar 45a) teaches, "There is a Temple in Heaven that is opened only through song."

Suggestions for Beginning the Exploration

- Try using a vocal tone during your prayer and meditation time. You can start with any word that is meaningful to you: "God," "Christ," "love," "peace," "om." Feel the vibration within your body as you chant. Do you feel any emotions come up? Afterward, reflect on your experiences.
- Explore possibilities for chanting in community, such as a Taize service (described later in the book). Pay attention to all aspects of your experience—including the emotional and physical—when you chant with others.

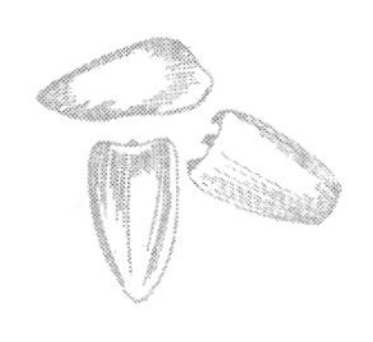

DESPACHOS

Offerings of Gratitude

Every good gift and perfect gift is from above,
coming down from the Father of the heavenly lights,
who does not change like shifting shadows.

—JAMES 1:17

Flower petals, candy, cocoa leaves, quinoa seeds, alpaca fat—this unusual combination of items includes some of the elements that can be found in the Andean shaman's ritual offering known as a *despacho.* Contained within a larger bundle, these little paper packets—each holding a single ingredient—are unwrapped ceremoniously by shamans who serve as priests or healers; each ingredient signifies a particular blessing of life. Unwrapping the *despachos* is sometimes accompanied by a communal ritual in which each member breathes their good intentions for another into a handful of cocoa leaves, then exchanges them as tangible markers of their prayers for the other.

Gathering symbolic items to represent blessings or as prayers for a good life is a practice that is echoed in a variety of cultural forms—such as the tiny protection packets carried in Mexico and Peru to bring good fortune. In both countries, the red Huayruru seed is included for luck, and both add depictions or symbols of saints—in Mexico, San Martin Caballero, known for his charity to the poor; in Peru, a broom that symbolizes San Martin de Porres, a black saint from Lima who is honored as a protector of both children and the impoverished throughout Latin America. Wheat seeds in the Peruvian good-luck packet are added to attract an abundance of food. The magnet or *Piedra Iman* in the Mexican protection packet is to attract luck.

Similar to these are the doll-sized Peruvian and Guatemalan vials that are made by folk doctors or *curanderos*. In the Guatemalan vial one might find mustard seeds, to protect one against all harm; *piedra de ara,* a gray stone that attracts money; and *flor de Hermano Pedro,* or "flower of Brother Pedro," a brown flower that cures the sick. Saints' images are included to achieve different results: San Antonio will improve one's love life; San Judas will help with business; San Simon or Maximon—a Guatemalan folk saint—can help one quit drinking or smoking.

In the Peruvian amulet vials, one might find minerals to attract money; colored tree bark for health; and, for those who have lost a lover or friend, a curled yellow vine called "Vuelve, Vuelve," which helps the bearer to regain the lost relationship. Every amulet vial also includes a carved, painted alabaster figure of a saint, each of whom plays a different role in the realm of life. A brown figure represents Saint Francis, the patron saint of animals; a yellow figure, Saint Cyprian, the patron saint of healers; blue, Saint Anthony, the patron saint of lovers.

A skull represents protection of the home; a closed hand represents the *Mano Poderosa* of Christ, which also protects. A white figure represents the child of knowledge or wisdom.

These colorful traditions of symbolic ingredients inspired Caterina Rando, a motivational speaker, writer and life coach, to do something special to celebrate her thirty-fifth birthday. As she had spent the preceding New Year's holiday period in Peru at Machu Picchu, where she was a part of rituals in which shamans unwrapped *despachos*, Caterina invited three of her closest women friends to participate in a unique outdoors celebration—she had brought back a *despacho* from her millennium journey to Peru for just this occasion.

Caterina created a sacred space by placing a blanket from the Sacred Valley of the Incas on the ground to acknowledge Spirit and that we are all spiritual beings. She circled the area with seashells brought back from Sicily, the home of her ancestors. Caterina tied a purple ribbon around each of the women's wrists, to acknowledge them as her soul sisters, walking with her and guiding her. She also sprinkled bay leaves around—substituting for the cocoa leaves used in Peru by shamans—and lit a candle. Then, the *despacho* was opened: a large bundle filled with smaller ones tied with string. One by one, the women took turns in opening the bundles and interpreting their contents to create prayers for Caterina. When a bundle containing sugar was opened, "May your life be full of sweetness" was the blessing; a bundle of confetti, "May your life be full of fun and festivity." Each time a bundle was opened, a pinch of the special contents was offered to the earth to honor the practice of the Peruvian shamans, from whom Caterina had learned about *despachos*.

"This was really a spiritual ceremony," remembers Caterina. "It was a ritual not only to celebrate my life but to set the intention for the cycle that was beginning, witnessed by the wise and influential women in my life.

"I loved the creation of it—selecting all the elements for it was very intentional. I felt it connected me to my Higher Power and the power within me. The most wonderful part of it was having everybody open the packets up and share their own interpretations and intentions—that was such a gift! It was wonderful creating my own personal, unique ritual and encompassing the *despacho* within that. I also loved *not* doing it how it was 'supposed to be done'—really making it my own thing was so much more meaningful and powerful for me than doing it the traditional way."

By shifting our focus to see all the gifts around us—and by noticing the spiritual messages we often receive through such symbolic representations as *despachos* offer, we can dramatically increase our sense of inner contentment. As the Sufi proverb notes, "Abundance can be had simply by consciously receiving what already has been given."

Suggestions for Beginning the Exploration

- Begin to think metaphorically about the everyday items that surround you. Could you see a coin you find on the street as representing your financial needs being met? Could coffee grounds represent something bitter being transformed into something that gives you energy? Can popcorn kernels represent the potential of something that explodes with excitement? Can you view sunflower seeds as something that nourishes on many levels, bringing forth both flowers and food?
- Wrap a few of these items in paper—choose beautiful colored or patterned paper, if you like—and place them in a bowl. When you are praying with a problem or a question, pick one of the small packets at random and open it. What might God be saying to you through it?

ELEMENTS

The Fourfold Roots of Everything

Hail to the Ocean! Hail to the wave!
The flood with holy fire to lave!
Waters hail! All hail the fire!
The strange event hail we in choir!
Hail light airs now floating free!
Hail earth's caves of mystery!
Held in honor evermore
Be the elemental four!

—JOHANN WOLFGANG VON GOETHE

In the fifth century, Empedocles, a Greek philosopher, healer, and scientist living in Sicily, devised a system that to this day has had ongoing reverberations. He conjectured that all matter is made up of four elements—earth, air, fire, and water—and that these elements are not only physical phenomena but spiritual essences.

Writing in his treatise, the *Tetrasomia* (Doctrine of Four Elements), Empedocles outlined the characteristics of these elements: fire and air reach up and out, and thus are outwardly focused; water and earth are inwardly focused, turning in and going down. In his philosophy, the two great energies of life are love and strife, and these influence the interaction among the four elements.

Since then, the philosophy of the four elements has influenced astrology, alchemical meditation, and Wiccan practice. Native Americans honor the four elements, seeing in them patterns for all of life: baby, child, adult, elder; physical, mental, spiritual, emotional. And though the concept of the elements developed in the West, it has its Eastern counterparts: in ancient China, the basic components were said to be earth, wood, metal, fire, and water. In India, the elements were proclaimed to be earth, space, air, fire, and water.

The elements have influenced the field of modern psychology, as well. The early Greek physician Hippocrates divided personalities into four humors—blood, phlegm, yellow bile, and black bile. Each of these humors represented different temperaments—enthusiastic, apathetic, changeable, brooding—which in turn have their relationship to, respectively, fire, earth, air, and water. It is presumed that Swiss psychologist Carl Jung's categorization of the personality into four components (intuition, sensation, thinking, and feeling) is derived from the theory of the elements.

This all connects to the spiritual with the understanding that one's inner development is related to the interaction among all the elements of the psyche—whether they are, to use Empedocles' terminology, existing together in love or strife. In astrology, each zodiac or sun sign is assigned to an element; there are fire, earth, water, and air signs. These each have corresponding qualities that will demonstrate the natural proclivities of a person born under that sign. For instance, Capricorns are an earth sign; as that element might imply, they are considered solid, conventional, prudent, and deliberate. Understanding the strengths and weaknesses of the element with which our astrological sign is associated—just as understanding which one of Jung's personality types, as popularized by the Myers-Briggs personality test, best represents us—can help us not only to embrace the totality of who we are but to identify those tendencies within us that may be in need of spiritual growth.

The important concept behind the elements is balance, honoring the whole—like the cycle of the seasons, which are also grouped into four. The number four has a myriad of associations; among the most important for a spiritual exploration are the four quadrants that are made up in a cosmic, or equidistant, cross. With the vertical line suggesting the spiritual plane and the horizontal line suggesting the earthly, as human beings we are called to be in that kind of balance—connected to the Divine of our understanding, while reaching out in service to the fellow human beings on our path.

In being aware of the elements, we can enhance our prayer life, as they also serve as metaphors for the necessary ingredients of a spiritual journey. As the Gnostic teachings remind us, "The earth is faith, in which we take root. Water is hope, by which we are nourished. The air is love by which we grow, and the light is Gnosis, by which we ripen."

Suggestions for Beginning the Exploration

- If you have a personal altar, try incorporating all four elements on it: a candle for fire; incense for air; a bowl of water; a rock, special crystal, or flowers to represent earth. Notice how interacting with these elements affects your prayer time.
- Choose one of the elements to focus on in prayer: light a candle and look into the flame, hold a rock or smell the fragrance of the flower, watch the smoke from the incense drift, bless yourself with the water. How do each of these deepen your understanding or experience of the Divine?

EXAMEN OF CONSCIENCE

Paying Greater Attention to What We Do

Without a searching and fearless moral inventory, most of us have found that the faith which really works in daily living is still out of reach.

—ALCOHOLICS ANONYMOUS' *TWELVE STEPS AND TWELVE TRADITIONS*

For many Baby Boomers who have abandoned their childhood faith traditions and have strong aversions to the word *sin,* it can be helpful to know that the original Greek wording refers to an archery term: "missing the mark." Who could feel badly about missing the mark occasionally? And it might be useful to frame it in the context used by writer Kathleen Norris to depict the approach of the Desert Monks: "They saw sin (what they called bad thoughts) as any impulse that leads us away from paying full attention to who and what we are and what we're doing; any thought or act that interferes with our ability to love God and neighbor." Viewed this way, the time-honored tradition of the Examen of

Conscience (a period in which one reflects on the impulses expressed during that day) becomes not a self-flagellating confession of perceived misdeeds but a soulful search of one's own actions—and whether they have moved the individual closer to, or farther away from, God.

In the late sixteenth or early seventeenth century, a Catholic monk from Spain named Alphonsus Rodriguez wrote these words:

> One of the chief and most efficacious means we have for our spiritual advancement is the examen of conscience; and for this reason the Saints recommend so earnestly the practice of it. Saint Chrysostom says that we should make this examen before we go to bed; and gives two good reasons for it. First, that the day following we may be the better disposed to preserve ourselves from the faults we have committed; for if we examine ourselves well over night, and conceive a great sorrow for our defects, and propose firmly to correct them, it is certain that this will serve as a curb to hinder us from falling into them again the day following. Secondly, the prospect of examining ourselves at night will be an occasion of greater recollection all the day long; for remembering that we have, on the very same day, to render an account of what we have done, will make us stand more upon our guard, and pay greater attention to what we do.

Rodriguez continues to explain that according to Saint Jerome and Saint Thomas, Pythagoras instructed his disciples "that they should daily, morning and evening, employ some time in examining themselves upon these three questions: What have I done? How have I done it? What have I omitted to do? He further bade them to rejoice at what they found they had done well; and repent, and feel sorry for what they had done amiss. Seneca, Plutarch, Epictetus, and many others recommend the same thing."

The Greek philosophers were not the only ones advocating self-examination and subsequent self-correction; in the Old Testament, the honorable Job asks, "How many wrongs and sins have I committed? Show me my offense and my sin" (Job 13:23). According to Confucius' *Analects,* "The Master said, 'In vain have I looked for a single man capable of seeing his own faults and bringing the charge home against himself.'" Jesus said that "there will be more rejoicing in heaven over one sinner who repents than over ninety-nine righteous persons who do not need to repent" (Luke 15:7). And what is repentance? According to Joseph B. Soloveitchik, author of *Halakhic Man,* "The desire to be another person, to be different than I am now, is the central motif of repentance."

While religious authorities have always played a role in determining which actions constitute a move away from God—perhaps most particularly in the Catholic Church, in which penitents receive absolution after their confessions—the ability to examine one's own heart is a powerful commodity. "A humble knowledge of thyself," wrote Thomas á Kempis in *The Imitation of Christ,* "is a surer way to God than a deep search after learning."

One of the many contributions that the tenets of Alcoholics Anonymous have brought to twentieth-century culture is a modern interpretation of the Examen of Conscience, known in Twelve-Step circles as Step Ten: "Continued to take personal inventory and when we were wrong promptly admitted it." This personal inventory can range from the "spot check," which can be done at any time; the inventory of the day's events at night; the occasional inventory done with another, such as a sponsor or spiritual advisor; and those undertaken during solitary retreats. It is important to include in the inventory the things we've done *right*—as *Twelve Steps and Twelve Traditions* suggests, any inventory includes both debits and credits. Do this, and the reward—while simple—is sweet: "Having so considered our day, not omitting to take due note of things well done, and having searched our hearts with neither fear nor favor, we can truly thank God for the blessings we have received and sleep in good conscience."

Suggestions for Beginning the Exploration

- Before going to sleep, review your day. Are there any things that you would like to do more skillfully next time? Are there any amends or apologies that you need to make?
- Track how doing this practice affects your spiritual life. Notice if it helps you to feel closer to God, closer to people, or closer to yourself.

FASTING

Days of Uninterrupted Prayer

She or he who does good of her or his accord shall be rewarded, but to fast is better for you, if you but knew it.

—MOHAMMAD

In a society in which consumerism reigns and advertisements constantly beckon us to get more, more, more, the concept of fasting can be hard to embrace. We have become object and information junkies, used to immediate gratification and stimulus. Fasting—abstinence not only from food but from anything that invites obsessive attention or satisfactions found outside of God—is a foreign concept for most people, something done long ago by people of different religions and not something applicable to the fast-paced world of today.

But more and more people are returning to the practice of fasting, both to enhance their physical health and to purify their spiritual health. Practitioners of fasting believe that because it disrupts one's daily patterns of scheduling meals and receiving the attendant pleasure from eating, it forces people to call upon their own inner resources when that pleasure is abandoned. For when all distracting temptations are removed, one must turn one's attention to God.

Fasting has been a part of religious life since antiquity, having been practiced by the early Egyptians, Mongolians, Syrians, and Mayans. Siddhartha Guatama fasted forty-nine days under the bodhi tree to achieve enlightenment and thus become the Buddha; Moses, Elijah, and Jesus Christ all fasted for forty days. Fasting is related to prayer in both the Old and New Testaments; in one example, the connection is made for us—a worshiper is said to have "never left the temple but worshipped night and day, fasting and praying" (Luke 2:37). And Christian scholars have noted that in the New Testament, there is more teaching by Christ on fasting than on repentance, confession, or baptism.

Other world religions and cultures have incorporated fasting into their faith practices in even more significant and established ways. Jews fast during Yom Kippur, Hindus fast on certain days of the month, such as on the full moon Purnima; and Native Americans fast before going on vision quests.

And spiritual leaders aren't the only ones who extend their fasts for weeks or even months. Today, Muslims fast during Ramadan, eating only after sundown and before sunrise; and Bahá'ís observe a month of fasting that precedes their New Year. In *Selections from the Writings of 'Abdu'l-Bahá*, an important Bahá'í spiritual teacher, the author instructs, "This material fast is an outer token of the spiritual fast; it is a symbol of self-restraint, the withholding of oneself from all appetites of the self, taking on the characteristics of the spirit, being carried away by the breathings of heaven and catching fire from the love of God."

In Islam, fasting is thought to be a special form of worship; it would be easy to sneak a morsel or two when no one's looking, and Allah is the only One who will know if you are really abstaining. It is also believed that fasting is a shield, an act of spiritual devotion that will protect the person from other sinful acts.

In Hinduism, fasting is done to deny physical needs for spiritual gain. Hindus believe that because of worldly distractions, believers must impose their own restraints upon their behavior to stay focused on the spiritual. One famous Hindu, Mahatma Gandhi, described a 1930 fast as "twenty-one days of uninterrupted prayer," concluding that "there is no prayer without fasting!" And Gandhi's prayer practice had political repercussions; he used his fasting as a form of nonviolent protest.

Hindus are aware of the Ayurvedic benefits to this practice; fasting releases built-up toxins that can cause disease. And Western proponents of fasting say that the practice induces clarity of mind, gives additional energy, and provides a sense of satisfaction that the body has been cleared of toxins. Even more important, a prayer practice of fasting can build compassion by reminding us through our pangs of hunger of the experience of those who have no food.

Encouraging the use of "penitential fasting," particularly in those countries whose inhabitants not only enjoy plentiful stores of food but also suffer diseases from overeating, Pope John Paul II wrote, "Penitential fasting is obviously something very different from a therapeutic diet, but in its own way it can be considered therapy for the soul. . . . One of the meanings of penitential fasting is to help us recover an interior life. The effort of moderation in food also extends to other things that are not necessary, and this is a great help to the spiritual life. Moderation, recollection, and prayer go hand in hand."

And in the Protestant Christian tradition, there is a modern "Fasting and Prayer Movement" that is gaining popularity. On one of the group's Web sites *(www.fastingprayer.com)*, they explain, "Fasting is a means of humbling ourselves before God, letting Him know that we are willing to exchange physical comforts to seek Him for a spiritual feast. . . . Fasting is the act of abstaining from feeding the body in order to focus more fully on seeking God's face and feeding the spirit."

It is that last point that lies at the heart of fasting; we fast to establish a closer communion with the Divine, and constantly communing in prayer during a fast is an integral element of the spiritual process. Geoffrey Chaucer may have summed up the practice most efficiently when he wrote in *The Canterbury Tales,* "Whoso will pray, he must faste and be clean, / And fat his soul, and make his body lean."

Suggestions for Beginning the Exploration

- Start slowly—first try skipping a meal, and spend the time you would normally be eating in prayer. Then, extend your fast—choose a day on which you won't be working to devote to fasting, and feed your spirit instead. How does a day spent fasting affect your spiritual experience? (With certain health conditions, fasting can be dangerous; do not attempt to do a prolonged fast without supervision.)

- Consider fasting from any substance that is detrimental to your spiritual experience—it could be television, action movies, romance novels, recreational shopping, or gossiping. Continue to choose new things to "fast" from.

FEASTS

Savoring the Sense of Interconnectedness

Enjoying a sumptuous, elaborate meal with others is one of life's greatest pleasures. As you dine, savor the sense of interconnectedness of all life: yourself, family and friends, those who grew, harvested, and prepared the food, and the food itself.

—DEBORAH KESTEN

Although the word *feasts* in religious contexts usually refers to the faith tradition's calendar of significant annual events or the major communal rituals held within each year, feasting as a prayer practice can be viewed much more simply and universally. As writer Mary Caswell expressed in *The Art of Tradition: A Christian Guide to Building a Family,* "What makes mealtime so important? Eating is a physical act, but it is also a spiritual act. It nourishes both body and soul. In utero we are fed by our mother's body. As infants, we are nourished by milk from her breast. From the beginning, as we partake of food, we partake of relationship. . . . The emphasis is on sharing: sharing food, sharing thoughts, sharing stories. . . ."

Around the world, people share food in their spiritual communities, often partaking of foods that serve as significant symbols. In the Hindu tradition, coconut and mango represent the sacred and auspicious; and during the butter festival in Tibet, held on the fifteenth day of the first moon, sculptures of Tibetan deities are carved out of butter by Buddhist monks. In the Jewish tradition, bread and slices of apple dipped in honey signify a wish for sweetness in the new year, while eggs have been used in the pagan tradition to symbolize fertility (and later were brought into the Christian feast of Easter). And in the Christian tradition the concept of a feast is perhaps taken to the highest symbolic extreme, in the form of Holy Communion. When Jesus broke bread and shared wine with his disciples for the last time, he counseled them to repeat the act in memory of him, saying that the bread was his body and the wine was his blood. While some Christians believe this literally, and others metaphorically, it remains a powerful image for those who include this practice in their spiritual activities.

Perhaps not surprisingly, feasts and deities have always been connected; most festivals were originally held to celebrate the Divine beings that people have worshiped throughout time. There is even biblical precedent for it: According to Leviticus 23:1–2, "The Lord said to Moses, 'Speak to the Israelites and say to them: These are my appointed feasts, the appointed feasts of the Lord, which you are to proclaim as sacred assemblies.'"

Feast days are a universal impulse of the human spirit to mark the important days of their spiritual passages. A feast becomes a prayer practice when it honors the sacred and acknowledges the transcendent. In earlier eras of humankind, feasts were held in accordance with the seasons, celebrating the planting and the harvesting—something we still celebrate, though perhaps in a more secular fashion, during the American Thanksgiving. The word *holiday* has its roots in the words "holy days," and holidays still celebrate the holy the world over. Just a quick sampling of feast days held by different religious or ethnic traditions include the Ukrainian Feast of the Baptism of Jesus in the Jordan (January 19), the Irish Feast of Saint Brigid (February 1), the Chinese Religious and Civic Commemoration of Ancestors (April 5), the Japanese Kodomo-No-Hi, or Children's Day (May 5), and the Native American Kateri Tekakwitha (July 14).

Two religious feasts in the Muslim calendar promote thinking of others. Eid Al Fitr, the festival of fast breaking after Ramadan, is a three-day celebration in which Muslims give a charitable gift to the poor. During Eid Al Adha, the festival of sacrifice, a cow, sheep, or goat is killed; the meat is shared by friends and relatives and is distributed to the poor. During both feasts, gifts are distributed among children, and sweets and other special foods are exchanged. Both feasts are marked by early-morning prayers praising God. Visits to friends and relatives include asking for forgiveness for any wrongdoings of the previous year.

In addition to the feasts that are held in community, we hold personal feasts on dates that are significant to us: our birthdays, our weddings, our funerals. The Hindus mark the birth of a baby and the transition into puberty with a feast.

The act of gathering together in intimate groups and larger communities affects our lives on a number of levels, enhancing our understanding of and identification with our family, our religion, our culture, and our country.

Besides the meaning behind and participation in the feast itself, there are other spiritual considerations related to food, such as the practice in Orthodox Judaism of keeping kosher—only allowing in their home foods that are "clean" according to ancient spiritual laws and thus can be consumed. In the Catholic tradition in the United States, meat was prohibited on Fridays until 1966; now Catholics must avoid meat only on Ash Wednesday and on the Fridays during Lent. Despite the relaxation of their dietary restrictions, Catholics still avoid ingesting any food or beverages for one hour before taking communion.

Muslims also have dietary laws that are a matter of faith, and Hindus generally avoid all foods thought to hinder spiritual development, including meat; many Hindus are vegetarian because they don't want to inflict harm on another living creature. Beef is never eaten because the cow is considered sacred; however, the products from cows—such as milk, yogurt, and ghee (clarified butter)—are considered innately pure.

Buddhists' customs vary; many Buddhists are vegetarians, but some believe that they may eat meat if they did not personally slaughter the animal.

Given the differences in approach to feasting, perhaps only one thing can be used as a universal guideline: To be a prayer practice, feasting should not incorporate gluttony. Many spiritual leaders would agree with the following counsel from Bhagavan Das: "If you have too much of anything, you cannot know yourself."

Suggestions for Beginning the Exploration

- To use a kitchen term, consciously "fold" prayer into your cooking time. As you prepare a meal, pray for those who will be eating the food.
- Pay attention to the colors, textures, and tastes of the food you're preparing or eating. How do they remind you of the Sacred? Use your feast celebration as a time to savor the sweetness—and the saltiness—in your life.

Food Meditations

Staying Mindful of the Mystery

This ritual is One.
The food is One.
We who offer the food are One.
The fire of hunger is also One.
All action is one.
We who understand this are One.

—Hindu blessing

If humans do not live by bread alone, how ironic that in an age of spiritual hunger, more Americans are overweight than ever before. Popular psychology tells us that food can be a substitute for love or comfort—but knowing that does not necessarily lead to a change in behavior. By looking at eating as a sacred act—as every act of our lives is, potentially—we can begin to shift our emphasis from living to eat to eating to live.

The spiritual reasons for doing so are many—first and foremost, because most faith traditions hold that the Divine is a part of us. In the New Testament, this concept is expressed succinctly: "Don't you know that you yourselves are God's temple and that God's Spirit lives in you?" (1 Corinthians 3:16). Additionally, we are called to remember that food is a gift from God. In another example from the New Testament, Jesus models what our approach to food should be: "Then he took the seven loaves and the fish, *and when he had given thanks* [emphasis added], he broke them and gave them to the disciples, and they in turn to the people" (Matthew 15:36).

This, then, becomes the next step in a spiritual approach to food; after acknowledging that we are the temple of God, we give thanks to God for the food that we have to eat. This simple act makes our eating conscious, allowing us the opportunity to apprehend what we are blessed to have and ensuring that we won't take it for granted. (There is a bit of theological controversy around this point that should be noted: Some people, when saying a grace or blessing before their meal, ask that the food be blessed for their health, good use, and service to others. In response to this practice, others have noted that it's not the food we're meant to bless—our focus should be on God.)

What follows after expressing gratitude is the act of eating itself. It is here that the Eastern concept of mindfulness can make this act a prayer practice, a present-moment meditation of awareness of all the abundance in one's life. As Jon Kabat-Zinn explains in *Full Catastrophe Living*, "When you eat mindfully, you are in touch with your food because your mind is not distracted. It is not thinking about other things. It is attending to eating.... Knowing what you are doing while you are doing it is the essence of mindfulness."

And mindful eating not only benefits the individual; it can also be shared with our companions at the table. Vietnamese Buddhist monk Thich Nhat Hanh, who has offered a number of approaches to mindful eating, explains one of its benefits: "If someone is thinking about something other than the good food on the table, such as his difficulties in the office or with friends, it means he is losing the present moment, and the food. You can say, 'This dish is wonderful, don't you agree?' When you say something like this, you will draw him out of his thinking and worries, and bring him back to the here and now, enjoying you, enjoying the wonderful dish. You become a bodhisattva, helping a living being become enlightened."

But even more powerfully than that, Thich Nhat Hanh helps us to see that consuming anything that is not for our highest health and good is detrimental not only to ourselves, but to all of society. He points out that a number of elements are toxic to us—that not only can foods poison us, but also violent television programs or movies, books and magazines, and even conversations. We start by being mindful of the food we eat, but to continue our path of spiritual development and awareness, we must extend our mindfulness to all of the things we consume in our lives. As he writes in the Fifth Precept of the "Diet for a Mindful Society," found in his book *Touching Peace,* we transform the primal urge to eat into a spiritual intention to serve when we vow "to ingest only items that preserve peace, well-being and joy in my body, in my consciousness, and in the collective body and consciousness of my family and society." Most important, he suggests, a proper diet will not only transform the individual both physically and spiritually—it has reverberations that affect the whole and is crucial "for the transformation of society."

Suggestions for Beginning the Exploration

- Before eating, have a moment of silence or say a prayer in appreciation of the work of others to bring the food to your table.
- Do nothing else while eating; simply immerse yourself in the experience of tasting, chewing, and swallowing your food. Notice the colors, the textures, the smells.
- Eat slowly, chew carefully, and pay attention to how you are eating. Put your fork down between bites. Instead of eating a forkful of peas, try eating one pea at a time. Notice how your experience of food is different when you do this, and if eating mindfully helps to connect you to the Divine.

Forgiveness Practices

An Easing of Our Own Hearts

Forgiveness is an embrace across all barriers, against all odds, in defiance of all that is mean and petty and vindictive and cruel in this life.

—Kent Nerburn

Forgiveness. The word derives from the Old English *gifan*, to give—and when we forgive, we do indeed bestow a gift not only on the forgiven, but on ourselves. Forgiveness is a concept found in every major world religion. In the Jewish tradition, it is said that "the most beautiful thing a man can do is to forgive wrong"; while the Sikhs take it one step farther: "Where there is forgiveness there is God himself." What is forgiveness?

For some, it is acknowledging the other as a mirror. American sage Benjamin Franklin is reported to have asked, upon hearing why one person despised another, "What did you do to him that makes you hate him so?"—making the point rather bluntly that what we find unforgivable in others we might just find within ourselves. For others, it is patience in the face of receiving one's karmic due. According to Tibetan monk Khenpo Karthar Rinpoche, "In Buddhist philosophy and teaching, it is said that even your enemies are to be seen as your most helpful friends. You should be most grateful to them because they have given you the best opportunity to practice patience.... If you are afflicted by disease and a prominent physician comes, bringing the most modern and effective medical treatments, it would be incredibly foolish to try to get rid of him or to try to kill him. On the contrary, you should extend the warmest of welcomes toward him."

While we might be able to appreciate these concepts in theory and from an intellectualized distance, it is harder to be detached in the face of raw pain and injustice. From this perspective, forgiveness becomes—as spiritual teacher and author Jack Kornfield writes—"an easing of our own heart and an acknowledgment that, no matter how strongly you may condemn and have suffered from the evil deeds of another, you will not put another human being out of your heart. We have all been harmed, just as we have all at times harmed ourselves and others."

While forgiveness practices are work for all of us, for Ilene Cummings—a retreat leader, educator, and process specialist—forgiveness *is* her work. Ilene has chosen to explore forgiveness with others as a professional and spiritual path; she regularly conducts forgiveness workshops and is currently writing a book on the subject. Ilene's special interest in forgiveness developed when a prayer partner asked if Ilene had forgiven her ex-husband. Ilene hadn't. "I was shocked to realize that after all the spiritual work I'd done, I still hadn't forgiven him," she remembers. "So for the next two months, I worked on it—and it 'took' and held. After that, I found that I organically had compassion for him—and then a deep love, which I'd never had in thirty years. That's the way the heart works—forgiveness releases the constricted heart when it passes from 'I hate you' to the ultimate Christlikeness.

"We have to push all our patterns, all our roles, everything, away in order to forgive, and that's such a tall order. It drops everybody down to that deep inner voice. It's a transcendent experience; it becomes a prayer practice. We need to understand another definition of forgiveness—that forgiveness is the spiritual masterpiece of your life. It's not about who does what to whom; it's our natural state. It's not about the other person; it's about our own transformation. After all, you don't have to forgive. It's a choice."

As Ilene puts it, forgiveness is not about "putting whipped cream over the garbage." Keep in mind that forgiveness is not about condoning an action; it is about releasing yourself from negative feelings and memories. And, as nineteenth-century German novelist Jean Paul Richter reminds us, it's also about expressing our spiritual self, for "humanity is never so beautiful as when praying for forgiveness, or else forgiving another."

Suggestions for Beginning the Exploration

- If you are as yet unable to pray to forgive someone, start smaller—pray for the desire to pray to forgive someone.
- Think of a person whom you feel wronged you, then imagine that person as a child, or as a little baby. Feel your emotions soften. Stay with the image long enough to sense the sweetness and vulnerability in that person, that which is good.
- Reflect: Are there any times in your life when you did something similar, though perhaps on what you see as a smaller scale? Sometimes our anger at others is a projection of dismay at our own actions.
- Do research on some of the groups that are emerging around the world to promote forgiveness, such as Archbishop Desmond Tutu's Truth and Reconciliation Commission. Sometimes seeing what others have been able to forgive can inspire our own hearts to soften.

Formal Prayers

A Place to Begin

Lord, teach us to pray.

—Luke 11:1

For many people, reciting formal prayers is the full or final component of their prayer life; for others, formal prayers are a wonderful place to begin. Whatever they are for you, formal prayers link us to the lineage of our religious communities, who have been reciting the same prayers, sometimes for centuries. (The *Kyrie Eleison*—"Lord have mercy"—that is still sung in twenty-first-century churches has been used as a prayer-poem in worship since the fourth century.) Formal prayers also provide a common thread for current acts of public worship; formal prayer is a great unifier. Great joy can be found in closing one's eyes and listening to the myriad tones and timbres of voices reciting the same prayer, bonding with each other in the holy moment of the present.

In Christianity, formal prayer began with the example that Jesus Christ gave when asked how we should pray—the Lord's Prayer. Indeed, this model is held by some as evidence that we should only hold to formal prayer constructs, that Jesus' instruction was clear—we were given a formula, not an invitation to say whatever we feel like at the moment. Latter-Day Saints follow a repeating pattern when praying, which is done at the beginning of the day and at the end: Praise and thank God, ask for daily needs, ask to forgive, to be forgiven, and to resist temptation.

Prayers, recited in Hebrew, are required three times each day for observant Jews; they are to be recited with *kavanah,* a mindset of concentration and intention. Those who adhere to this say that the requirement ensures that people will make the time to communicate with God and retain awareness of God's presence and role in their lives. Additionally, it is believed that the practice that results from regular prayer will make you a more effective pray-er.

Formal prayer books have been in existence for centuries; the Book of Psalms is a collection of formal prayers, as is the Book of Common Prayer. One can also find prayer cards with prayers on them, as well as increasing numbers of prayer collections organized into particular themes.

Why do most religious institutions use formal prayer in worship services? Advocates say that it's helpful to keep worship orderly; that with formal prayer, people are less likely to bring up personal issues or veer off track to the detriment of the church community. Additionally, formal prayer can be helpful to alleviate feelings of self-consciousness or concern that one does not know the "correct" way to pray; it also helps tap into the wisdom of others who have found words to articulate challenging or complex topics and to give you additional insights into the subject matter of the prayer.

But perhaps formal prayer's greatest contribution is as a place to begin, a format to hold on to when our prayer lives are dry or difficult. The repetitive aspect of formal prayer can help create a container for our experience of God, serving as a form of intention and focus. Starting with an opening phrase of a well-known prayer can serve to open us up. It can be the beginning of our individualized expression of angst or awe.

Suggestions for Beginning the Exploration

- Choose a formal prayer that you have known since childhood. Be with it in a different way—say it slowly, reflecting on each word; write it out in a journal, pausing after each line. Is the prayer still meaningful to you, or has it lost fire through its familiarity?
- During your prayer and meditation time, try recreating that formal prayer by alternating its lines with lines of your own—write the first line of the prayer, then add a line of your own in response. Observe if interacting with it in this way brings it new life.
- Read the formal prayers of spiritual traditions other than your own. Watch what speaks to you, and think about ways to bring that phrase or concept back to your own tradition.

God Boxes

Counting Our Blessings, Letting Things Go

I am God. Today I will be handling all of your problems. Please remember that I do not need your help. If life happens to deliver a situation to you that you cannot handle, do not attempt to resolve it. Kindly put it in the SFGTD (something for God to do) box. It will be addressed in My time, not yours. Once the matter is placed into the box, do not hold onto it. . . .

—Internet chain letter by unknown author

There is something compelling about creating a container for the Divine; because the holy is ineffable and mysterious, perhaps we can begin to embrace it only when we're able to shape it—sometimes literally—into a form we can put our hands around. Prayer boxes are found in various cultures; prayers and sacred relics are kept inside Tibetan, Indian, and Turkic prayer boxes, which are made of silver and carried like a portable shrine. In Thailand, you can find boxes wrapped in Buddhist prayer scripture; you'll also see prayer boxes—often inlaid with the *om* or some other spiritual symbol—to keep prayer beads in. These are all precursors of the modern practice of keeping a "God box," which serves as a container for—and sometimes a record of—communications with the Divine.

God boxes probably derived from church prayer boxes, in which congregation members put their prayer requests to be retrieved later by church officials or volunteers and prayed over. This practice in turn has inspired Internet prayer boxes, in which you place your prayer request on an organization's or individual's Web site for those people to pray for you.

And in today's wired world, the practice of using a personal God box is spreading; do an online search for those words, and you'll end up with several versions of a poem, written by an anonymous author, that tells the story of God giving two boxes to the poem's narrator—one gold (to hold her joys), and one black (to hold her sorrows). As the gold box becomes heavier by the day, the black one remains as light as ever—and the narrator soon discovers a hole in its bottom, though which her sorrows fall into God's hands.

Whether you keep two God boxes or just one, there are a number of ways you can use them. Peg Grady, a pediatric nurse, school and church volunteer, and mother of three, says that using her God box is "a very important part of my practice now." Her box, roughly five inches square and made of inlaid woods of different colors and textures, is topped with a lid that depicts a butterfly—an important spiritual symbol to Peg. She says that using the God box emerged from her practice of keeping a prayer journal: "I expanded that to the box."

Peg continues, "In my box, which is on my downstairs

altar, I include the names of people I'm praying for, as well as prayers for myself—especially things I'm having a hard time letting go of. I've found that taking out and writing on a piece of paper and putting it in the box was a very concrete way of letting go and giving it to God.

"I write on tiny little pieces of paper; occasionally I'll go through the box. If the prayer has been answered, it turns into a prayer of thanksgiving. I keep a candle burning on my altar by the box when I'm at home during the day—it calls to mind for me that my whole life is a prayer; that every moment is a prayer."

Some people choose not to pray about their challenge after they have written it down and turned it into their God box, feeling that this is a way of showing their trust that the problem will be handled. Most people keep the slips of paper inside the box so they can later look through and see how their prayers have been answered; it is a visual way of proving that things that once seemed overwhelming have been lived through successfully. You can put a prayer request on one side of the paper, and on the other side write the date and situation when your prayer is answered. Keeping those spiritual records can be a comforting reminder that the Divine is always at work in your life.

You can also use a God box as a form of affirmation, writing down things that you desire to see manifested in your life on separate pieces of paper and then picking one out every day—and thanking God in advance for bringing that to you. Other people like to write God a letter, sign it, and place it in the box. After sitting in the silence for a moment, they then write a response to their own letter and put it into the God box. There are many variations on this theme; holding your prayers, desires, and dreams is a process that can be as creative as each person who practices it.

Perhaps the best-known user of a God box is writer Anne Lamott, who has written of her practice both on salon.com and in her bestselling book *Traveling Mercies*. As with every spiritual exercise, its ways are mysterious and rewarding. Writes Lamott, "It was just a little wooden box someone had given me once, that I'd decided would be God's in-box. . . . I don't understand why it would hurt so much if just once in His life, He used a megaphone. But He never does. I find this infuriating. But what happens when I put a note in the God-box is that the phone rings, or the mail comes; and I hear from Him that way."

Suggestions for Beginning the Exploration

- Look around for an empty box to use, cover a shoe- or cigar-box with paper, or buy a box to use as your God or prayer box. Write down your prayers and place them in the box; as you place them within, surrender that prayer to the Divine. Notice how physically writing your prayer down—and surrendering it to a physical place—impacts you.
- After you have done this for some time, read through your old prayer requests. What were the results? How have you grown?

GRATITUDE AND PRAYER JOURNALS

Recognizing the Gift as Gift

A grateful thought toward heaven is of itself a prayer.

—GOTTHOLD EPHRAIM LESSING

In her bestselling book *Simple Abundance,* author Sarah Ban Breathnach recommended a practice that has captured the imagination of many Americans, including Oprah Winfrey: keeping a gratitude journal. The influence of both women's work has helped to spread the word of the emotional and spiritual benefits of this practice, which are life changing, according to Breathnach. She writes, "You simply will not be the same person two months from now after consciously giving thanks each day for the abundance that exists in your life. And you will have set in motion an ancient spiritual law: the more you have and are grateful for, the more will be given you."

Three years after *Simple Abundance* was published, in a 1998 Gallup poll, more than 90 percent of Americans said that expressing gratitude made them happy—something that has been borne out by scientific research. According to those who have found this practice meaningful, cultivating an "attitude of gratitude" appears to affect one's life on every level—physical, mental, and spiritual.

The concept, while enjoying a modern renewal, is a time-honored one; sages throughout history have commented on the need to express gratitude. In *Androcles,* Aesop proposed that "gratitude is the sign of noble souls"; Seneca believed that "he that urges gratitude pleads the cause both of God and men, for without it we can neither be sociable nor religious." In the New Testament, we are reassured that all things work together for good (Romans 8:28) and that in all circumstances we should give thanks (1 Thessalonians 5:18).

Seeing the expression of gratitude as a prayer practice, fourteenth-century Dominican mystic Meister Eckhart believed that "if the only prayer you ever say in your entire life is thank you, it will be enough"; and former Secretary General of the United Nations Dag Hammarskjöld created a powerful prayer of gratitude and openness when he wrote, "For all that has been, thanks. To all that will be, yes."

Gratitude is the essence at the heart of all spiritual work: seeing what has been given to you, no matter how surprising or painful, as a gift for your soul's growth. And in the times when it is challenging to see any semblance of meaning or purpose behind one's travails, the habit of keeping a gratitude journal can be the discipline that sees us through—that takes us out of our raw hurt and into conscious awareness. Writing down what we have to be grateful for engages our mind, creating another cord to hold the heavy. As Brother David Steindl-Rast writes, "A single crocus blossom ought to be enough to convince our heart that springtime, no matter how predictable, is somehow a gift, gratuitous, gratis, a grace. We know this with a knowledge that goes beyond our intellect. Yet our intellect shares in it. We cannot be grateful unless our intellect plays its role. We must recognize the gift as gift, and only our intellect can do that."

There are many ways to keep a gratitude journal, which—if you prefer—can be a part of a spiritual or prayer journal in which you keep a record not only of the things for which you are grateful, but also note the cycles of your spiritual journey. In a prayer journal, you can write down insights and reflections, copy down prayers or passages from spiritual books that nourish you, or record your prayers, keeping note of what you pray for and how you witness your prayers being answered.

If you decide to keep such a journal, you'll be following a practice that has inspired some of the world's great leaders, including Moses (in Exodus 24:3–4, we learn that "Moses then wrote down everything the Lord had said"). Many centuries later, George Washington kept a prayer journal, in which he recorded the deepest desires and struggles of his heart.

To begin, schedule a regular time to spend with your journal, whether it's daily, weekly, or monthly. Choose a journal that you will enjoy holding and handling, and one that you feel honors the purpose for which it's being used. Begin your journal time with prayer and meditation.

Practitioners of spiritual journaling liken the process to writing a love letter to God, but underscore the need to be authentic when writing. Feigned holiness obscures the point, which is to stay in a state of gratitude by proclaiming gratitude.

It helps to hand-write your journal rather than type it into a computer; that personal touch adds to the feeling of communion and sacred time. One way to express your gratitude is to write down what you are grateful for (try including one thing each day that you've never mentioned before). Or, if you want to focus your journal more specifically, try keeping a list of all the things you're grateful for about yourself (or God): for example, that you're a good business person or that God is available to you.

Possibilities other journal-keepers have used include following a formal prayer as a format for your entries—echoing the content of each line. For instance, when using the Lord's Prayer, after "Give us this day our daily bread," you would write down your personal needs; after "Forgive us our debts, as we forgive our debtors," you would write down how you have missed the mark and who you need to forgive. You can also follow the format Catherine of Siena used in the late fourteenth century and described in *The Dialogue,* the book she dictated while in an ecstatic state—writing down a problem or question, then, after spending a moment in silence, writing down what God's answer might be.

Whichever form you use, you will want to make sure that gratitude is a big part of it, even during those dark nights of the soul. Why? In her magazine, *O,* Oprah Winfrey quotes Maya Angelou, who gives us the answer: "'You're saying thank you,' Maya said, 'because your faith is so strong that you don't doubt that whatever the problem, you'll get through it. You're saying thank you because you know there's no problem created that can compare to the Creator of all things. Say thank you!'"

Suggestions for Beginning the Exploration

- Start by writing down one thing you're grateful for at the end or beginning of each day; later increase that number so that you are creating a daily list of what you are grateful for. Notice how listing your blessings increases your awareness of them.
- If you'd prefer, start a prayer journal. Keep a record of your prayers, as well as a list of the results of those prayers; write down meaningful quotations that you gather from your spiritual reading.
- If you're visually minded, make a gratitude collage, or add pictures found in magazines, postcards, or letters from people you love to your gratitude journal.

GUIDES

Here to Help Us from Other Dimensions

Spirits
I can see
They will come to me
They will come down under a cloud
They will be my masters
I can see
They will walk in Raven town

—SAXA OF THE TLINGIT

Throughout the ages and in every culture of the world, people have believed in spiritual guides. From Native American and Aborigine tribes who communicate with animal spirits to the community of Catholics who call on guardian angels and saints, belief in and reliance on spirit guides is universal. Accordingly, there are as many thoughts about spirit guides as there are potential forms of spiritual guidance.

Depending on what culture you come from, there are different categories of helpers from other realms, including relatives or ancestors; angels (although some believe that angels, because of their different energy "vibrations," fall into a category of their own); master teachers; spirits (people who have died); *devas,* or nature spirits; and animals. Beyond that, some people have classified guides even further: There is the protector, who will keep you from harm; the gatekeeper, who at your request will allow around you only those energies that contribute to your highest good; the healer, who will assist with physical healing (some forms of Reiki—a natural method of healing based on Universal Life Force Energy, which is what the name translates as—encourage practitioners to get in touch with their guides); the philosopher, who provides wisdom; and the master teacher. Others have distilled the forms of help from other dimensions down to three categories: ancestors, animals, and angels or other spiritual guides.

Prayer is considered an integral part of contacting guides, as it creates a sacred environment and calls upon the Highest Power to be present. Guides are not worshiped; they help in divining Divine will, strength, and understanding. Some people see guides as aspects of our higher self that haven't as yet been incorporated into our everyday consciousness.

How does one communicate with guides? Again, the possibilities are as wide as are the beliefs. A guide can communicate with you through your intuition, that "little voice" in your head; in meditation, by answering the questions you ask; in automatic writing; through dreams; when creating (for instance, your guide might be a musician and give you the gift of songwriting); through telepathy; and through synchronicity.

Those who work with guides say that their presence is felt through a somatic experience: goosebumps, sudden bursts of emotion, beams of light, sounds, smells, a "knowing." It is believed that how your guide appears to you will probably depend on what form is most comfortable for you to perceive them and in what form you are most likely to listen to them. Sometimes you'll receive a name for your guide, sometimes not; sometimes you'll see your guide, sometimes you won't. Perhaps, as some believe, the "imaginary playmates" of children are actually their spirit guides—access to which is lost as they are told not to pretend.

Those who use spirit guides say that there is always help standing by; that whether the guide is an angel, animal, ancestor, or other spirit, there is access to guidance every hour of the day. Though some believe guides only assist you when they are requested to, others believe that sometimes they will intervene on behalf of your intentions. And it is believed that spirit guides are ours for life; even if we discount or ignore them, they are here to help us with our lessons and will stay with us throughout our course on Earth. Spirit guides are here to look after our well-being in every dimension of living.

Animal guides, or totems, on the other hand, illuminate for us qualities that we need to embrace or strengthen within our own personalities. When a particular animal comes to you in a dream or continually crosses your path, you might do research to find out more about the animal's qualities and what it might be trying to teach you. Shamans work with animal spirits, seeing them as allies. Native Americans, particularly the Zuni tribe, create animal fetishes, which are not to be worshiped themselves, but are to be used as a conduit for encountering or even embodying the spirit behind the representation.

Rituals are wonderful ways to call in ancestors; in the Mexican Day of the Dead festival, held annually at the beginning of November, celebrants honor ancestors by building offering altars, or *ofrendas,* laden with the favorite foods and beverages of their late loved ones. And some people believe that their ability to practice an ancient or esoteric craft is a result of one of their ancestor guides instructing them.

When exploring the subject of spiritual guides, it is recommended that you be in good health and have clean, orderly surroundings, which will result in higher vibrations and thus higher spiritual forms. Begin with prayer and ritual; be sure to draw in your higher spiritual teachers and do a protection prayer that invites only beings of light to enter.

While we incorporate the acknowledgment of our guides into our prayers, we are not praying to them—we are calling upon their energies and wisdom to be all that we are meant to be. The guides can assist us on our path, but cannot force action or events; the choices are ours. Those who work with guides advise not only respecting the guides, but also trusting them—as you would any friend. And the final thing to remember: Whether you work with guides or not, at the heart of your prayer practice, the Divine of your understanding remains the ultimate Spirit guide.

Suggestions for Beginning the Exploration

- Set up an altar that pays homage to your ancestors. On it, place their photographs and items that they once used: a teacup, a pair of glasses, a watch chain. Like with the Mexican *ofrendas* during the Day of the Dead, you might also add items that you know your ancestors loved: a bottle of beer, a box of chocolates, a can of mixed nuts. Journal about how this remembrance of your ancestors affects your spiritual experience.

- Look around—do you have a collection of animals around you? Are you drawn to a particular animal—is there one that you always rush to see at a zoo or animal park? Do you live with animals? Do you have animals appearing in your dreams? Note if there is any particular animal that keeps coming up for you, then read about it and study its habits. What does it symbolize for you?
- If you don't already have a physical representation of that animal, find a photograph, figurine, or piece of jewelry that you can place on your altar or wear. Notice how the qualities of this animal affect your spiritual understanding.

HAIKU

Expressing the Hidden Glimmering

Live in simple faith
Just as this trusting cherry
Flowers, fades, and falls.

—ISSA

The writing of haiku is a discipline, literarily speaking; most schoolchildren at some point in their education are exposed to the short poetic form from Japan that illustrates a seasonal scene in three lines, with a pattern of five, seven, and five syllables per line. It is a communication whose success depends on the lack of the subjective "I"; one of Japan's most noted haiku artists, Basho—who lived in the seventeenth century—had this to say about haiku: "Your poetry issues of its own accord when you and the object have become one—when you have plunged deep enough into the object to see something like a hidden glimmering there."

Haiku has its origins in the practice of *tanka,* which were incantations to gods, or prayers, that followed a five/seven/five/seven/seven syllable count and were popular in Japan in the ninth through twelfth centuries. Through the years, *tanka* practice evolved; the original author would stop after the first three lines, and another would respond by adding the final two. Others would respond in kind, and *tanka* sometimes had thousands of linking verses penned by other poets. From those initial three lines, the form of haiku was born.

Because of the differences between the Japanese and English languages, there is some debate as to what constitutes the appropriate discipline for contemporary English haiku. While some still adhere to the five/seven/five syllable construction in three lines, others argue that form allows for too much extraneous material when using English. As a result, some haiku writers follow a three/five/three syllable construction or put the emphasis on accented words (two/three/two). Generally speaking, there is agreement that the haiku should be three lines long; contain a seasonal word (either a direct reference or implied one: blossoms, snow, frog, leaves); refrain from intellectualizing or philosophizing, and focus instead on direct perception; and consist solely of words that are integral to the expression. But haiku teacher and author William Higginson got to the heart (and soul) of the matter when he wrote, "The primary purpose of reading and writing haiku is sharing moments of our lives that have moved us, pieces of experience and perception that we offer or receive as gifts."

John deValcourt, a professor of mathematics, was first drawn to haiku because of the inherent discipline imposed by following the seventeen-syllable form, as seventeen is a significant number in mathematics for several reasons, including being a prime number. His first foray into haiku was "sort of organic," he says; he wrote one for his son's seventeenth birthday, and from there, "they just emerged."

"They came out of meditation," John explains. "I would get up very early in the morning, sit silently, and they would just emerge. Some thought or insight would come into my mind, and I would write about it. That's how they became prayer, from how they came to me and what was in them.

"There was a certain facility that seemed to take place; maybe it was because they are short, and I could finish them almost at the same time I had the insight. That sense of almost immediate completion was an important aspect of the experience."

John calls these creations "prayku," noting that they differ from classical haiku because there is a personal reference to them—"and that's the whole point," he says. "I'm breaking the rules for a reason." One of the haiku that John wrote during this two-year practice of writing several haiku a week is this one:

> How long must we walk,
> eyes cast down, before we know
> our divinity?

And John has found his haiku prayer practice stretching; he has written haiku for others, which serve as tangible representations of his prayers for them. When a good friend was diagnosed HIV-positive, John gave his friend seven spiritual haiku written especially for him. John's gift is a good reminder that, as a prayer practice, everything and anything is appropriate to write about. As haiku teacher and writer J. W. Hackett counseled, "Life is the fount of the haiku experience. So take note of this present moment."

Suggestions for Beginning the Exploration

- Try incorporating writing haiku into the time of day that works best for you—early morning, during a quiet lunch break, before you go to bed. Sit quietly, and spend a few minutes simply breathing. When a thought, insight, image, or memory comes to you, pick up your pen and jot down the essence of it. Then, begin to craft your words into the haiku form of your choice, focusing either on the number of syllables in each line (five/seven/five or three/five/three) or on the number of accented words (two/three/two). Experiment, and stay with the format and content that helps you to best express that "hidden glimmering."
- You might want to keep your pieces together in a special journal or make a box or folder just for your haiku, using Japanese paper.
- As you continue this practice through one season and enter another, take stock: How has this practice deepened your experience of the Divine?

ICONS

Painted to Lead Us to the Heart of God

Icons . . . are created for the sole purpose of offering access, through the gate of the visible, to the mystery of the invisible. Icons are painted to lead us close to the heart of God.

—HENRI J. M. NOUWEN

Their look is singular: penetrating almond-shaped eyes, faces often encased in silver and crowned with gold-disk halos. The word *icon* comes from the Greek word for "image," and icons, pictorial representations painted on wooden panels, only image religious themes. Yet what one sees when looking at an icon is not meant to be a depiction; as writer and monk Thomas Merton expressed it, "What one 'sees' in prayer before an icon is not an external representation of a historical person, but an interior presence in light."

Dutch priest Henri J. M. Nouwen, in his book *Behold the Beauty of the Lord: Praying with Icons,* elaborates on this concept. He writes, "Icons are not easy to 'see.' They do not immediately speak to our senses. They do not excite, fascinate, stir our emotions, or stimulate our imagination. At first, they even seem somewhat rigid, lifeless, schematic, and dull. They do not reveal themselves to us at first sight. It is only gradually, after a patient, prayerful presence that they start speaking to us. And as they speak, they speak more to our inner than our outer senses. They speak to the heart that searches for God."

The origin of icons is not exactly known; according to legend, the first icon was made when a king, dying of leprosy, sent a message begging Jesus to visit and cure him. Since Jesus was journeying toward Jerusalem and his impending crucifixion, he sent a gift imbued with healing powers instead: a fabric image of his face.

The first painter of an icon is considered to be the apostle Luke, whose subject was Mary. Yet late in the seventh century icons were condemned by the church as "deceitful paintings that corrupt the intelligence by exciting shameful pleasures," as the Quinisext Council worded it in 692—while still recognizing icons as being helpful "to expose to the sight of all what is perfect." The Iconoclasts—those who wanted to destroy the icons on the charge that they were idols—had their way in the sixth century, when the pope, Emperor Leo III, ordered the removal of public icons. Yet iconography was later revived, enjoying its renaissance age during the fourteenth, fifteenth, and sixteenth centuries in Russia—a place that continues to inform the use of icons even today. To the Russian Orthodox Christian, icons are reminders of God's presence, and they are honored in special displays within the home, called the *krasniy ugol* or beautiful corner.

Indeed, it is felt that if one is really to pray with icons, one should live with them—and Jim Forest, author of *Praying with Icons,* suggests that one should have an "icon corner." Writes Forest, "Because icons are physical objects, they serve as invitations to keep our eyes open when we pray," and "It is prayer just to look attentively at an icon and let God speak to you."

Praying with icons has a number of levels; not only do we pray with icons once they are completed, but the artist incorporates prayer into the actual making of them. Indeed, the level of ritual and thought behind an icon's creation is deep. Icons are not signed because it is believed that God is the real artist. When an artist "writes" an icon, he or she is to have prepared for the task through prayer, fasting, and meditation, so that the image is revealed, not imagined. In other words, any element of fantasy or imagination is strongly discouraged by Orthodox Church leaders, to guard against worshiping an object of human—not holy—inspiration. Thus what we see in an icon is meant to be a portrait of the spiritual reality, not an exact likeness of the physical reality.

Yet, paradoxically, it is an important part of iconography that Jesus Christ, in particular, is represented in physical form. As the monk and poet Saint John of Damascus, whose life spanned the turn of the seventh to eighth centuries, said in response to whether or not icons were idolatrous, "Since the invisible One became visible by taking on flesh, you can fashion the image of him whom you saw. Since he who has neither body nor form nor quantity nor quality, who goes beyond all grandeur by the excellence of his nature, he, being of divine nature, took on the condition of a slave and reduced himself to quantity and quality by clothing himself in human features. Therefore, paint on wood and present for contemplation him who desired to become visible."

Icons, then, become a part of a chain of prayer, which begins with the artist before the icon is created and continues as the icon is made. When the icon is completed, it becomes a means to establish a prayerful environment—and, perhaps, a portal into a Divine dimension.

Suggestions for Beginning the Exploration

- Go through books that depict icons, or buy a book such as Henri Nouwen's *Behold the Beauty of the Lord: Praying with Icons* or Jim Forest's *Praying with Icons.* What images are you drawn to? Be mindful of your physical and emotional responses.
- Try creating a prayer corner with photographs or images that stir your soul. Pray in front of them, and notice how your prayer life is affected through this practice.

IKEBANA

The Way of the Flower

Where better than in a flower, sweet in its unconsciousness, fragrant because of its silence, can we image the unfolding of a virgin soul?

—OKAKURA KAKUZO

Though the practice of ikebana, the highly disciplined Japanese form of flower arranging, may not be associated immediately with prayer, there are reasons why we might make such an association. According to Okakura Kakuzo, author of *The Book of Tea,* "Our legends ascribe the first flower arrangement to those early Buddhist saints who gathered the flowers strewn by the storm and, in their infinite solicitude for all living things, placed them in vessels of water."

Other scholars concur that ikebana—which means "arranging flowers" in Japanese—has spiritual roots, pointing out that in the sixth century, ritual flower offerings began to be performed in Buddhist temples. An important component of the arrangement was the positioning of its elements: both the flowers and branches used were deliberately pointed upward to indicate the arranger's faith.

There is a face behind this faith practice; it is believed that ikebana was inspired after a Japanese man named Ono no Imoko traveled to China in the sixth century, later returning to Japan to become an abbot. During his travels, he had been introduced to the practice of arranging flowers as a religious offering, and he continued the practice even after he retired. There are a number of schools representing different forms of ikebana; the oldest of them is said to have developed from Imoko's practice.

These schools emerged beginning in the fifteenth century with *rikka,* a style of flower arrangement that reflected its name, which means "standing flowers." This school encouraged flower arrangement that depicted the Buddhist symbol of the universe, Mount Sumeru. Seeking to reflect nature's grandeur, the style was highly symbolic and sophisticated, yet today is obsolete. Still, Zen Buddhism and its symbolism remain a strong influence on the practice of ikebana; all arrangements are constructed with elements that represent heaven, earth, and humankind. A mindful arrangement brings these three components together when a human takes the flowers from the earth to represent the qualities of heaven.

Ruth Grosser, a Western ikebana artist, commented on both the practice's origins and effects when she wrote, "Ikebana has influenced many artists. The Samurai and Zen Masters discovered the essence. Your mind and body are relaxed. The whole self is centered on the art."

In fact, it is that aspect of ikebana—losing oneself in the act of creation—that inspired two writers to explore ikebana as a form of prayer or meditation. In their book *The Japan-*

ese Way of the Flower: Ikebana as Moving Meditation, authors H. E. Davey and Ann Kameoka express it this way: "Working with concepts such as these [in ikebana] requires a consideration of the nature of time and its meaning in our lives. Bringing the mind into the moment and observing ourselves in the moment is the essence of meditation—it allows us to enter into a state with no past and no future. In this everlasting moment, we find no birth, not death, not time, and no fear."

Furthermore, the authors point out, there is nothing like a prayer form dependent on elements that will soon wither and die to reinforce the concept of—and practice of—nonattachment. Their response to those who wonder at the fragility of these spiritual tools? "These individuals have failed to realize that the very fact that flowers do not last is what makes arranging and viewing them special," write Davey and Kameoka. "These same folks suffer from the illusion that some form of permanent art exists. It does not. Beauty is in the moment, and realization of its fleeting nature is what encourages us to live every instant completely, with our whole minds and bodies."

Whether one follows a particular school of ikebana as a spiritual discipline, or simply decides to view flower arranging as a visual form of prayer, there are many metaphorical associations that will enrich our practice. After all, the lotus is the symbol of spiritual unfoldment in the Buddhist tradition, just as the rose is spiritually significant in the Christian tradition. Perhaps that is because, as Luther Burbank wrote, "There is no other door to knowledge than the door nature opens; there is no other truth except the truths we discover in nature."

Suggestions for Beginning the Exploration

- What flowers are you drawn to—what flowers represent the spiritual life to you? Begin by placing these on your altar or in the place where you pray and meditate.
- Try expressing different attributes of the Divine through flower arrangement. What would majesty look like? What blossoms would you use to depict mercy? Compassion?
- *The Language of Flowers* is a classic little book that explains the folkloric meaning behind flowers—for instance, rosemary signifies remembrance. Being mindful of the meanings of flowers can add another dimension of significance to The Way of the Flower when using it as a prayer practice.

INSTRUMENTAL MUSIC

Symbolizing the Yearning for Harmony

Prayer is the world in tune.

—HENRY VAUGHAN

Though instrumental music is a part of worship in traditions all around the world, it was not always so. In the Christian church, especially, whether or not to accompany public worship with music has been a source of debate for centuries—and even today some churches do not use instrumental music because they do not believe that Jesus Christ sanctioned its use in worship.

Despite a scriptural verse that encourages its use—"Speak to one another with psalms, hymns, and spiritual songs. Sing and make music in your heart to the Lord" (Ephesians 5:19)—music did not appear in Christian church worship until the sixth century; organs were first used in Western European churches in the seventh century. Why this resistance to something that so many believe lifts one's heart to heaven?

Italian theologian Thomas Aquinas answered this question with this response: "For such like musical instruments move the soul to pleasure rather than create a good disposition within it." And early Christian philosopher Augustine stated his opinion even more strongly: "The pipe, tabret, harp here associate so intimately with the sensual heathen cults, as well as with the wild revelries and shameless performances of the degenerate theater and circus, it is easy to understand the prejudices against their use in the worship."

In other cultures, there are echoes of this concern; for example, Buddhist monks may engage in performing religious music, but do not do any secular singing, dancing, or playing of instruments because of the sensual nature of these practices. Within Buddhist worship, however, music plays an important part; monks chant scripture and play ritual instruments, the latter primarily to mark the passages of worship. Even visually, instruments play a role: the ritual scepter and bell represent aspects of enlightenment—compassion and wisdom—in Vajrayana Buddhism. Buddha himself, using a musical image, taught, "A small bell in a mindful and loving hand wakes up thousands of sorrowful beings."

In India, instrumental music has been used for prayer throughout history, and there are Hindu deities who are affiliated with music. Saraswati, who plays a string instrument, is the goddess of music; Krishna plays the flute, Shiva carries a drum and wind instrument, and Vishnu carries the conch, known as a *sankha,* which is associated with prayers.

In all cultures, music can be used as a way of altering perceptions; in shamanic journeying, the steady rhythm of drums, bells, and other instruments can transport the hearer into another world of perception. The phenomenon known as "entrainment" links its listeners physiologically, as a rhythmic cadence invites bodies to beat to the same pace.

Music can be used as a form of offering or an attempt to convey the majesty of the Divine; who hasn't had their breath taken away by the music of Bach? And playing instruments can also be used as a form of prayer practice, a way in which to commune with the Divine.

Growing numbers of people are seeking to promote greater appreciation and understanding of the role of spiritual music; one organization devoted to the task is the World Festival of Sacred Music. In a statement made for the WFSM, His Holiness the Dalai Lama wrote, "Among the many forms in which the human spirit has tried to express its innermost yearnings and perceptions, music is perhaps the most universal. It symbolizes the yearnings for harmony, with oneself and with others, with nature and with the spiritual and sacred within us and around us. There is something in music that transcends and unites. This is evident in the sacred music of every community—music that expresses the universal yearning that is shared by people all over the globe."

Suggestions for Beginning the Exploration

- Is there a piece (or pieces) of music in which you experience the Sacred? When did you first have that experience? Do you feel the same things now when you hear the piece as when you first heard it? While listening to it meditatively, note the words, phrases, or feelings that arise.

- Explore praying with music in the background and praying in silence. Does one deepen your experience more than the other? How do they differ? Is that difference always the same?
- Try playing an instrument as you pray—whether it's the piano, a flute, a rattle, drum, or rainstick. Notice if actually contributing music adds to your spiritual experience.

LABYRINTHS AND PRAYER-WALKING

Metaphors of Our Spiritual Journey

*All those who walk with God reach
their destination.*

—SAI BABA

For more than 4,000 years, people have been walking some form of labyrinth; the religious traditions incorporating its use range from Native American to Greek, Celtic to Mayan. Turf labyrinths honoring the feminine can still be found in Europe; they are at least a millennium older than the birth of Christianity.

The Christian use of labyrinths flowered during the Middle Ages; labyrinths still exist at Chartres and other cathedrals in France and Germany. They were an important substitute when people were not able to make a pilgrimage to the Holy Land; a symbolic representation of that journey, they sometimes were created out of natural materials such as stones, sand, and flour.

Unlike circumambulation, which is walking around a sacred site, labyrinth walking focuses on what's being walked on. The labyrinth has been compared to an umbilical cord, and as such it offers no dead ends; it is not like a maze of the English-garden variety. There are three predominant labyrinth designs, each with a certain number of circuits: seven, eleven, and twelve.

According to the Rev. Lauren Artress, author of *Walking a Sacred Path: Rediscovering the Labyrinth as a Spiritual Tool* and the person widely credited with the recent reemergence of the labyrinth as a popular prayer practice, the labyrinth is a metaphor for our lives—how you "do" the labyrinth is how you "do" life. For example, will you step off the labyrinth to let others pass, or do you stand firm so that others must make way for you?

And, like every day of our lives, each time we walk the labyrinth we'll have new perspectives. Our experience of the labyrinth can be enriched through bringing different concerns to it; we can use it as a vehicle to work with a question, grapple with a need to forgive, or simply calm and recollect ourselves. We can walk on it barefoot, dance or skip along its circuits; we can track how our step changes as we enter it and as we go out. Some have postulated that labyrinths can shift our consciousness and balance our energies because of the movements required to walk it, accessing both our right- and left-brain functions.

As a mirror of our spiritual journey, there are three stages to our experience of the labyrinth: purgation, in which the details of everyday life are released; illumination, the place of meditation and prayer; and union, joining God and being strengthened for our work in the world. Circular in format, the labyrinth is entered through an opening that then loops back and forth as one follows its intricate winding way to the center. One exits the labyrinth by the same circuitous path—though if the journey is done mindfully, the return route will not seem redundant.

In addition to the labyrinth, there are other forms of prayer practice that involve walking, including the kind of walking meditation taught by Vietnamese Buddhist monk Thich Nhat Hanh. Like other forms of mindfulness meditation, the intent behind walking meditation is to use our breathing to connect to the present moment, to find the joys inherent in the here and now, and to spread them by holding this peaceful presence within. Thich Nhat Hanh makes the point beautifully when he asks us to remember that "it is no miracle to walk on water. It is a miracle to walk on this Earth."

Another form of moving practice referred to as "prayer-walking" is approached in a variety of ways. In the 1970s, this informal Christian movement began: practitioners would choose an area in which to walk, then pray for the people they encountered, as well as for the unseen people living in the houses they passed. This form of prayer-walking was sometimes done in teams, taking as inspiration such Bible verses as Psalm 25:4 ("Make me to know your ways, Lord, teach me your paths") and Isaiah 30:21 ("And when you turn to the right, and turn to the left, your ears shall hear a word behind you, saying 'This is the way, walk it'").

Other forms of prayer-walking are done in solitude, for the purpose of communicating with the Divine. Suggestions for using this time include asking God to show you something relevant to whatever concern you're facing, giving gratitude to God for the beauty you see around you, praying for those who are in special need, sending out loving energy to the rest of the world, or simply moving through angry or fearful feelings. As Linus Mundy, author of *The Complete Guide to Prayer-Walking*, puts it, prayer-walking is "an exercise that considers and serves every part of the human being: the mind, the body, the spirit (or soul). It is prayer-exercise that makes it possible for us to look inside and outside of ourselves simultaneously."

For Joan Currey, associate director for outreach at San Francisco Theological Seminary who also leads small pilgrimages to cathedrals in France, it is that physical aspect of walking the labyrinth that is deeply important: "It gets your whole self in alignment with prayer. It takes a little while to even get into the rhythm—and then you sink into the right rhythm for yourself. Getting the body involved seems to make it a more whole prayer time—particularly if it's uncomplicated, so you don't have to focus on the movement itself. It literally fleshes out the prayer—without that, something seems to be missing."

Walking centuries-old labyrinths, such as the one at Chartres, is deeply satisfying to Joan: "It has such a long tradition—it's like going to a place that's been prayed in a lot; there's a sense of the prayers being still there. It's as if it has been soaked in prayer, as if the ground has already been tilled for you. And it raises the question: Did God bring people there because it's a holy place, or did people make it that way because of prayers, or is it both?"

When Joan has finished a labyrinth walk, she makes sure later to spend time with her experience: "With any of these prayer experiences, it's the reflection afterward that can broaden and deepen it—it was T. S. Eliot who said, 'We had the experience but missed the meaning.' So I always take time to reflect on it afterward—it's then like a bell that has been struck and rings on and on and on."

Suggestions for Beginning the Exploration

- Try a mindfulness meditation while walking. Pay attention to each movement of your body, as you repeat a phrase of spiritual significance to you.
- Use a neighborhood or nature walk as an opportunity to pray for all you encounter along the way.
- Try prayer-walking on a labyrinth. To find one in your area, visit: *www.gracecathedral.org/labyrinth/locator/index.shtml*

MANDALAS

The Path to the Center

*I saw that everything, all paths I had been following,
all steps I had taken, were leading back to a single point—
namely, to the mid-point. It became increasingly plain to me
that the mandala is the center. It is the exponent of all paths.
It is the path to the center, to individuation. . . . I knew that
in finding the mandala as an expression of the self I
had attained what was for me the ultimate.*

—CARL GUSTAV JUNG

An ancient spiritual art, mandalas have a history that stretches back for centuries, emerging as an important meditative practice in Hinduism and Buddhism, particularly Tibetan Buddhism. *Mandala*—the Sanskrit word meaning "circle"—is also a compound of the Sanskrit *manda,* meaning "essence," and the suffix *la,* "container." And indeed, many spiritual traditions around the world have created and meditated upon the mandala as a "container of essence."

Because of its primarily circular form, with an inherent center, the mandala is a symbol of wholeness. It is both a microcosm and a macrocosm; in it, it is believed, we can see ourselves—and we can see the universe. In the Hindu and Buddhist traditions, meditation on a mandala is said to promote the essential state of being that is only found when one encounters the Divine, that mandalas—and their geometric counterparts, yantras—are a doorway to Spirit. Though mandalas are all visual pieces, they are made in a variety of ways. In both the Tibetan and Navaho Indian traditions, impermanence is an integral symbolic component of the creation of mandalas; in these cultures, intricate mandalas are created out of colored sand and later destroyed.

Gail C. Jones is an educator, consultant, and spiritual director who has been drawing mandalas as a regular prayer practice for almost two years. "The idea of the practice of the mandalas came partly from learning that Carl Jung drew a mandala every day as a way to tap into his soul," Gail says. "And because my normal way of being is as a 'thinking type,' I need ways that help me get below the surface. For me, poetry and drawing have been a way to unlock the inner soul and to bring the insights into the light of day.

"Doing mandalas opened up a whole new facet of my being. Drawing gets into the collective unconscious—for example, I started a series of hearts with eyes in the middle of them. Later, I discovered that it was a symbol on medallions of alchemists in the fourteenth century: the eye of the heart. It was so incredible that something in me was part of something that was deeper and more ancient, tapping into something that is way below the surface.

"When we're working with spiritual exploration, we need

to work with art—to unleash that which is below the surface so that we can tap into the soul of the universe. When we look for perfection instead of wholeness, we get ourselves into trouble. This 'perfect' stuff has to do usually with what someone else thinks is perfect, instead of exploring how am I called out as an individual expression of God?

"The circle of the mandala is what's been helpful to me—there's a wholeness in the circle. It's an ancient symbol, throughout all cultures. There's something archetypal about that. I just sit down and draw the circle and wait for something to emerge. I give every mandala a title, and I've found that to be a very helpful practice—it's a very important discipline. Sometimes my images seem mundane to me—but so is our journey sometimes; our mandalas can reflect all aspects of our experience.

"Normally I'm intentional about doing it—I light floating candles, do journaling along with it, usually after doing a mandala. My primary prayer practice had been intercessory—reading Scripture and meditating around that. Now, instead of starting with a known thing, I start with myself. For me, it's a new path on the journey—I rely less on the written word and more on what my soul's saying."

Whether you explore meditating on classic mandala images, or choose to make them, as Gail does, you await a discovery. French humanitarian Albert Schweitzer could have been describing mandalas when he wrote: "Whenever we penetrate to the heart of things, we always find mystery. Life and all that goes with it is unfathomable. . . . Knowledge of life is recognition of the mysterious."

Suggestions for Beginning the Exploration

- Try making your own mandala, or keep a mandala journal. Pay attention to the symbols and colors that keep appearing in your mandalas. As Susanne Fincher suggests in her book *Creating Mandalas,* try assigning your personal meanings to every color and image that come forward. What do the color red, images of birds, a spiral shape mean to *you?* (Fincher also includes a section on the cross-cultural meaning of colors, images, and particular shapes.)
- For particular mandala practices, look through Judith Cornell's *Mandala.* In her beautifully illustrated book, she offers a number of meditative exercises to try.

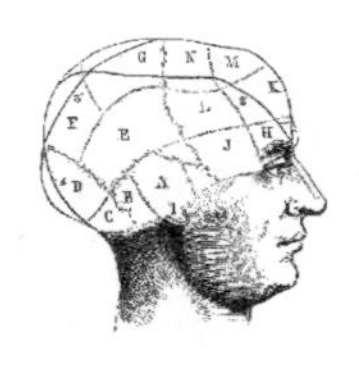

MASTER MIND GROUPS

Connecting with Infinite Intelligence

When two or more people coordinate in a spirit of harmony, and work toward a definite objective, they place themselves in position, through that alliance, to absorb power directly from the great universal storehouse of Infinite Intelligence. This is the greatest of all sources of power.

—NAPOLEON HILL

Master Mind Groups have corollaries with prayer gatherings and other support groups, informed by the New Testament verse in which Jesus said that "where two or three come together in my name, there am I with them" (Matthew 18:20). The modern manifestation of this kind of collective, the concept of a Master Mind Group, was birthed in the late 1930s by American author Napoleon Hill, who believed that the energy of a group, connected in mental focus and spiritual intent, becomes so great that it "penetrates to and connects with the universal energy."

Hill's belief in the power of a collective to bring its members to new levels of experience and understanding began when, commissioned by Andrew Carnegie to research hundreds of successful people and explore the reasons for their success, he discovered that many of them participated in some form of a "master mind" group. The phenomenon seemed almost to be magnetic; those groups whose members remained focused achieved extraordinary levels of personal and professional success. As Hill explained it, "When a group of individual brains are coordinated and function in harmony, the increased energy created through that alliance becomes available to every individual brain in the group."

While Master Mind Groups can be more secular or superficially oriented—just another self-development tool for garnering worldly success rather than deepening one's very experience of God—they also can be used as a powerful prayer practice. The late Jack Boland, a Unity minister from Michigan, took up where Napoleon Hill left off, creating a number of practical workbooks, planning calendars, and manuals from the Master Mind principles that Hill introduced. These are still being published by the Church of Today in Warren, Michigan, near Detroit, whose recent roster of ministers includes author and activist Marianne Williamson.

As the Church of Today explains in its written materials, "The Master Mind Principle is a scientific method of focusing the power of thought for the specific purpose of establishing a direct connection with the Master Mind.... Through the Master Mind Principle, you combine your own strength with that of at least one other person—as well as that of a Higher Power. The principle is based on an ancient premise that the combined energies of two or more like-minded persons is many, many times greater than the sum of the individual energies involved."

Toward that end, practitioners of the Master Mind Principle have suggestions for creating a successful Master Mind Group. The first is to keep the group relatively small; between two and seven people is considered an optimal number. The shared intent and focus of all members is extremely important, as is the willingness to support—and stay with—the process.

Though a facilitator is helpful for leading a Master Mind Group, all members of the group are considered equal—and the Master Mind, God, is acknowledged as the true leader of the group. As a Master Mind Group is a form of support group, members are to respect confidentiality and stay in touch with each other.

Master Mind Groups can meet once a week or once a month; they can gather in any environment conducive to their goals—a member's home or business, a restaurant or a church. Areas that Master Mind Groups might want to explore include purpose, prosperity, health, and happiness.

Once your group is in place, the Rev. Boland advised taking eight steps into the Master Mind Consciousness:

1. To surrender
2. To believe
3. To be ready to be changed
4. To decide to be changed
5. To forgive

6. To ask
7. To give thanks
8. To dedicate one's life.

Suggestions for Beginning the Exploration

- Think about people in your community who share similar values and with whom you feel comfortable. Who might make good partners in a Master Mind Group? Introduce them to the work of Napoleon Hill or Jack Boland, and form a Master Mind Group with those who are excited about exploring possibilities.
- What is calling—what do you need to dedicate your life to right now? Are there areas of your life that could be strengthened by having the prayer support of others? Discover the power of sacred intention by creating support structures—such as a Master Mind Group—that focus on particular issues in your life. Abundance, spirtual connection, and relationships are all possible themes.

Meditation and Breathing Practices

Inhaling the Spirit of God

Prayer is exhaling the spirit of man and inhaling the spirit of God.

—Edwin Keith

So much has been written about meditation and breathing practices that the newcomer who wants to begin meditating can be overwhelmed. In this context, spiritual teacher Swami Chetananda's comment about meditation is particularly helpful, as it uses a metaphor that puts this prayer practice into terms that everyone can understand: "When you are with someone you love very much, you can talk and it is pleasant, but the reality is not in the conversation. It is in simply being together. Meditation is the highest form of prayer. In it you are so close to God that you don't need to say a thing—it is just great to be together."

Although meditation is practiced in some form in every world religion, including Sufism, Islam, and Judaism, its predominant association is with Eastern religions, especially Buddhism. And when discussing meditation with those who follow the Christian path, there is an important semantic difference to be aware of: the distinction between *contemplation* (what Christians call the practice we refer to here as "meditation") and the Christian definition of *meditation*—a disciplined reflection on spiritual concepts and experiences.

In addition to differences in terminology, there are differences in the experience of meditation; meditation can result in a mystical experience of the transcendent or be a tool for escape from the mundane, depending on one's motivation and approach. There are also varying forms of meditation, including those that involve the use of concentration (repeating a mantra or word, such as in Transcendental Meditation or Centering Prayer); insight meditation, which helps the practitioner to develop greater mindfulness; and *zazen*, the sitting meditation of Zen, which aims to empty the mind, using the breath. As Thich Nhat Hanh writes, "If the lake of the mind is still, all wonders are reflected in there." The practice of meditation by Westerners began around the fourth century with the Desert Monks, who probably were influenced by the Eastern approaches found in Hinduism and Buddhism.

In the 1960s, interest in meditation was fanned again, and Westerners began adopting practices from Hinduism and Buddhism. The founder of Transcendental Meditation (TM), Maharishi Mahesh Yogi, asked scientists to study the effect of it on practitioners; those involved in meditation practice were shown to have more resistance to stress, lowered instances of illness, and higher levels of relaxation and feelings of well-being. This promoted a certain secularization of meditation; it was seen as a technique for stress reduction rather than spiritual practice. Those who use meditation as a spiritual practice would no doubt attribute its healing effects to its relationship in accessing God, transforming our everyday material existence into the felt sense of Spirit.

No matter which form of meditation you choose, whether you stare at a flame, count your breaths, or repeat a mantra, what's important—as with any spiritual practice—is the intention with which it's done and the desire to attempt it at all. Think of meditation as breathing your prayers, as creating the space to be in the presence of God, to know God—perhaps even to become one with God.

It has been said that meditation is about listening for God's voice, for guidance about moving through our lives. As the following story demonstrates, being conscious of our breath and using it to help us affirm "the highest and holiest" is also an important reward of meditative practices—even those that are momentary in duration.

A former nun, the Rev. Louise Dunn is an ordained minister and head of the now 270-member church that she founded in Indianapolis, The Church Within. Her schedule is filled with one-on-one meetings as a counselor and spiritual director, and for that deep, compassionate work, Louise has adapted a prayer practice that involves her breath.

"I use it when I'm with someone who is difficult, either to get along with or to understand," Louise says. "I call it the 'Three-Breath Blessing.' I will take three conscious, deep breaths and say silently, *Bless this moment,* repeating it with each breath. I know that my intention is to center in my God-self, so the breath and the blessing take me to a deeper level of listening.

"Because I'm going to a new level of being, the people I'm with respond. It's awesome in its effectiveness. Once I had a person, referred to me from another counselor, who was acting out a serious pathology—the energy given off by this person was pure hate. I used this prayer to shift the energy in the room and to start inviting the highest and holiest in that person forward.

"The personality didn't change, but this person started gentling down. Throughout that session, I kept repeating my practice—there is something about it that envelops me and the other person in the safety of Spirit. It's quick, and it could probably be done in just one breath—but three is such a spiritual number, I feel I need it.

"We live in an age of expectancy—we expect results instantly. There's been such a forward movement in our evolution as a species; technologically we're so fast, and we need the equivalent in Spirit. This is the quickest prayer practice in the world."

And perhaps we should keep this in mind when exploring meditation and breathing practices—that the fruit is found in the practice, and we can start by just doing it, rather than waiting until we've found the "right" technique. As the Buddha said, "It were better to live one single day in the pursuit of understanding and meditation, than to live a hundred years in ignorance and restraint."

Suggestions for Beginning the Exploration

- Try different ways of coming into stillness—watching a candle flame, repeating a word that has spiritual significance for you, paying attention to your breath. When your thoughts intrude, gently dismiss them and go back to your practice.
- Explore using your breath in prayer, as Louise suggests. The next time you are afraid or angry, try the "Three-Breath Blessing." What other areas of your life can you bring meditative or breathing practices into?

MILAGROS

Representations of Blessings from Heaven

We live today in a world that seems short of miracles,
a world where the miracles that do happen go unremarked.
Based on traditional Mexican talismans, the tiny, personal
charms known as milagros *remind us that miracles*
can be small, they can be numerous, and
they can happen every day.

—HELEN THOMPSON

They can be as small as a thumbnail, or as large as a heart, which is appropriate for a silvery image that represents a fervently said prayer. *Milagros* (Spanish for "miracles") are used primarily in the Mexican and South American cultures as tangible representations of a prayer of petition or a prayer of thanksgiving. Usually made out of silver, mixed metal, or tin, milagros are made in all shapes and sizes; the littlest among them are called *milagritos*.

Milagros probably have their origins in the practice of giving *ex-votos* ("from my vow" in Latin) or votive offerings to saints. When a prayer request was made to a saint, so was a vow—to carry out a particular action in return. To seal the spiritual deal, a token is provided, offered to the petitioned saint. The use of ex-votos, found at the temple of the healing god Asclepius, not only has been documented in classical Greece but is still practiced today in several countries, including Morocco, India, and Iran.

Milagros and their offshoots are also made in glass, pottery, plaster, wax, wood—even sugar. The sugar offerings, often found on altars in Peru and Bolivia, are called *mysteriosos* ("mysterious things") and are used to honor depictions of Ekkeko, the Andean god of abundance.

Yet the kind of milagros most often seen are those in the form of body parts—a leg, eyes, breasts. These milagros are used as prayers for healing the part of the body depicted—or as thanks for a healing that has occurred. Sometimes, the person who is praying will write the name of the person who needs healing, or even an entire prayer, directly on the milagro, but this detail is not considered a requisite one for receiving Divine aid.

In addition to parts of the body, you can find milagros that represent animals—used in prayers either to have the animal cured of an illness or to be purchased. Milagros also make reference to deities, such as the sacred heart of Jesus, and include images of people kneeling in prayer, as well as items in a person's possession that need to be protected.

Like the prayers that incorporate the use of them, milagros are made one at a time, and are made by a person, not a machine. You'll find milagros placed on altars or affixed to statues or other sacred symbols; since a recent wave of interest in milagros has occurred, they can even be found incorporated into jewelry. You can also buy crosses covered with little milagros, representing abundant blessings from above.

And don't let their small size eclipse their larger place in a prayer life. As author Helen Thompson writes, milagros "are symbolic of a covenant between a believer and a higher spirit, tangible testimony that a promise has been fulfilled. . . . Whether you look at their place in your life as a symbol that you are trying something new or as a means to focus yourself on a transition, milagros offer an alternative approach to spirituality."

Suggestions for Beginning the Exploration

- If you or someone you know is in need of healing, try praying with a small representation that symbolizes the object of your prayers. Does it help to have something tangible to hold onto or see?
- When you receive a blessing, try honoring it with a material image of thanks. For instance, you might buy a living plant to place in your prayer space.

PERSONAL SACRED TEXT

Prayer Crystallized in Words

Think truly, and thy thoughts
Shall the world's famine feed.
Speak truly, and each word of thine
Shall be a fruitful seed.
Live truly, and thy life shall be
A great and noble creed.

—HORATIUS BONAR

Without thinking about it, many of us have chosen a particularly beautiful or inviting journal in which to collect the poems, quotations, song lyrics, scriptural passages, and spiritual reflections that have touched us deeply. It is the beginning of a prayer practice that we can consciously employ: creating our own personal sacred text.

In his *Markings*, former Secretary General of the United Nations Dag Hammarskjöld writes, "Prayer, crystallized in words, assigns a permanent wave length on which the dialogue has to be continued, even when our mind is occupied with other matters." Assembling a book of the words that have moved us most, our own prayer book, does inform our lives even when we are otherwise occupied, for it stands as our declaration of what we hold most holy in the world, the cherished precepts by which we live.

Not many people have written about creating a personal sacred text; the one notable exception is author and therapist Bobbi L. Parish. In her book, *Create Your Personal Sacred Text: Develop and Celebrate Your Spiritual Life,* she walks the reader through defining a text, assembling it, making selections from existing material, writing personal scripture, and using it. In the first chapter, she encourages us to honor our uniqueness: "There never has been, and there never will be, another human being exactly like you. Your thoughts, personality, ideas, and behaviors will go unduplicated for all of time. Consequently, no one has or ever will again have the understanding of and relationship with Spirit that you do. Your work will have a value unequal to anything else that will ever be done."

As a singular creation, the possibilities for your text are endless. You are the scribe, divinely inspired by your God, and can include anything that nourishes your soul. Whether you use a Bruce Springsteen song or a Pierre Bonnard postcard of springtime pastels, passages from *The Cloud of Unknowing* or an image of Georgia O'Keeffe's painting of clouds, your personal sacred text will be a one-of-a-kind collage of the things that stir your spirit. In the making of your text, you will discover more about yourself; while you will probably refer to your text during your time of quiet and meditation, the creation of it is also a prayer practice in itself.

The outside of your prayer book can be as meaningful as the inside. *Spirituality and Health* magazine offered a free online cyber workshop on designing and creating your own sacred journal led by Sandra Kahn, a bookbinder in Cambridge, Massachusetts. In it, she provides inspiring ideas for decorating the outside of your text, along with exercises for approaching the inside.

One interesting way to approach the creation of your personal sacred text might be as a metaphor for your own life. As such, what you put on the cover might have more significance. This could influence the inside, as well. You might want to choose a journal bound with sections of different colored paper. Another option could be to use one of the popular notebooks consisting entirely of black pages on which you write with milky pastel gel pens, or, as Kahn suggests, make or buy an accordion-style book to represent your lifeline.

You can try to retrace your spiritual path chronologically, starting with the pieces that uplifted you as a child, teenager, and young adult through to the present, or you can categorize your text, using ribbons or bookmarks made of beautiful paper to divide your text into areas of focus. It helps to work on your text after spending time in prayer and meditation—remember that the object of this practice is not to try to make something look perfect, but to collect those elements that have represented a perfect expression of Spirit to you.

To begin to cultivate ideas for how to approach your sacred journal—particularly if you think you are going to include visual images—it might be fruitful to look through spiritual books that contain both text and illustrations. Some possibilities include the *Sister Wendy* series of meditation books; books of illuminated prayers, such as *Illuminated Prayers* by Marianne Williamson; *The Secret Language of the Soul: A Visual Guide to the Spiritual World* by Jane Hope; and two collaborations by translator Coleman Barks and collage artist Michael Green, *The Illuminated Rumi* and *The Illuminated Prayer: The Five-Times Prayer of the Sufis*.

Delight in the process as you sift through the colors and the quotations that have touched you through the years—or create your own as you are moved to in the moment. Use as your guidance the words of the great Sufi poet Rumi, who wrote, "Let yourself be silently drawn by the stronger pull of what you really love."

Suggestions for Beginning the Exploration

- Have you ever kept a notebook full of poems, quotations, or song lyrics meaningful to you—or do you now? If so, you have already begun creating your personal sacred text. If not, begin to pay attention to what moves you or inspires you as you go through life. Anything's appropriate—from a fortune-cookie proverb to a quotation on the inside flap of a box of tea—if it stirs you spiritually.
- As you begin to assemble a collection of words and images that are significant to you, comb through them—what do they say to you? Reflect on how they have changed your experience or understanding of God.

PRAYER BEADS

Touching the Holy

The beads! I hold in my hand a very humble little rosary. . . . Made precious because it has been with me through many hours of joy and sorrow, it is a constant companion, a sign of hope, a link with heaven, with heaven's Queen, our life, our sweetness, and our hope.

—M. BASIL PENNINGTON

When most people think of prayer beads, it is the Catholic rosary (usually made of colored glass or plastic beads, sometimes olive wood) or Buddhist *mala* (sandalwood, seeds, or inlaid animal bone) that usually comes to mind. But with the exception of Judaism, prayer beads are found in every major world religion as a means of counting prayers, and the practice today is undergoing a renaissance as spiritual seekers of no set tradition are incorporating them into their prayer lives in fresh and meaningful ways.

The ancient use of prayer beads originated in India with the Hindus, who used strings of 108 beads, worn around the neck, to count mantras. This tradition was later adopted by Buddhists in Tibet, China, and Japan, who also used 108 beads; Buddhist monks in Burma prefer to use a string of 72 black-lacquered beads. (In Tibet, *malas* of inlaid bone were originally made from the skeletons of holy men, as sacred reminders to live lives worthy of being elevated to the next level of enlightenment. Today's *malas*, sometimes inlaid with turquoise and coral, are made of yak bone.) Prayer beads are also used by Muslims, who use strings of thirty-three or ninety-nine beads, which represent the ninety-nine names of Allah found in the Koran.

Christian prayer beads developed in the sixth century, when Saint Benedict of Nursia asked his disciples to pray the 150 psalms of the Bible at least once a week. This assignment was too hard for some to commit to memory, and a substitution of 150 *Paters* ("Our Fathers") was allowed. Beads were used to count the *Paters,* and this string of 150 beads became known as a Paternoster. (There is an interesting side note in the origin of Christian prayer beads involving a woman who is known in cultural folklore for baring things other than her soul—Lady Godiva. According to her will, she established a convent in 1057 and bequeathed her beads of precious gemstones, which she used for saying Paternosters, to the convent upon her death—the first recorded mention of Christian prayer beads.)

Saint Dominic is widely believed to have introduced prayer beads as Christians know them today after a visitation by the Blessed Virgin Mary, and Thomas of Contimpre was the first to call them a rosary, from the word *rosarium* or rose garden. Indeed, strung rose petals have been used to count prayers, as have the knots in Byzantine prayer cords.

Today, this widely practiced and time-honored tradition is being given new life by people who are seeing previously unrealized possibilities for prayer beads. Given that the very word *bead* comes from the Anglo-Saxon *bidden* ("to pray") and *bede* ("prayer"), some people interested in updating this practice believe that it is appropriate to focus on the actual beads used as well as on ways to personalize their significance.

A wonderful example of how this can be done is found in the story of dentist Holly Downes. A twenty-year student of Buddhism, Holly made her first *mala* in response to an experience she had during a vision quest one summer. Gathering acorns from the base of the tree near which she camped, Holly strung them into a short strand of prayer beads when she returned home. Blending her Western professional training with her Eastern spiritual studies, Holly used dental gold to craft counting pieces: two tiny bees, with images of an endless knot carved on their bellies. Explains Holly, "During my vision quest, I stayed under an oak tree and noticed all this life in it: birds, butterflies, geckos running around the base and up it. I realized as I got quieter that I could hear humming in the tree—about fifteen or twenty feet up, there was a beehive. I kept watching two bees who couldn't make it back up; they were doing a death dance, walking on the ground away from the hive.

"At the time, I was looking at endings in my life. I realized that the Tree of Life is not only about life, but death—it's a continuing circle. The hive didn't stop, and my work will continue, as people come into and out of my life. Within an ending is a beginning. The acorns on my *mala* also symbolize this—these seeds of life are varied. Some are very, very tiny; some are big—they illustrate different phases of growth from that tree. The making of this *mala* was my prayer—to bring into the physical plane the learning from that experience, so that I can remember it."

As Holly's story illustrates, integrating personal symbols of significance into your prayer beads helps to enliven their use. Additionally, different numbers and colors have spiritual meanings in several cosmologies; if you want to try making your own prayer beads, some research into these properties may deepen your experience of creating them.

However, there are also makers of prayer beads who don't believe that there's any power in the elements themselves, but rather in the constant reminder prayer beads provide of the need to stay grounded and in touch with the Divine force that the beads acknowledge. Like their secular counterpart, the worry beads often used in Greece and Turkey, prayer beads offer kinesthetic comfort—they are a means in the material world to remember one's place in the spiritual world.

In addition to being part of one's private prayer life, prayer beads increasingly are being implemented in celebrations and rites of passage. For example, commemorating a milestone birthday with friends or family who each offer the gift of a colorful bead will result in a precious strand of prayer beads that will represent the many lovely textures of personalities, intentions, and relationships in the life of the person being honored. Other people have used the ritual of making prayer beads to commemorate weddings (by incorporating symbols and talismans of both families being united in marriage) and births (by having participants bring beads to represent the blessings they wish to bestow on the child).

Suggestions for Beginning the Exploration

- If you don't already have a rosary or *mala*, is there something you hold on to while praying—a charm on a necklace, a tassel on a bookmark? Consider incorporating that into a strand of prayer beads.
- Prayer beads can be bought or made; they can be long enough to place over your head, short enough to wear around your wrist or place in a pocket. Find the length that best supports your needs, and touch the beads as you pray. Notice how the tactile influences the spiritual in your life.

PRAYER BOWLS

Vessels That Invite Us to Enter the Sacred

The twenty-four elders fell down before the Lamb,
each holding a harp, and with golden bowls full of incense,
which are the prayers of the saints. . . .

—REVELATION 5:8

Whether called a prayer bowl, a blessing bowl, an offering bowl, a prayer cup, a cup of life, or a chalice, a vessel with a round, open shape is an invitation to enter the sacred. When the bowl is just the right size, one can place one's hands around it; held in such a way, one can begin to see it as a metaphor for one's life. As Joyce Rupp, author of one of the few books on this topic, *The Cup of Our Life: A Guide for Spiritual Growth,* writes,

> The cup has taught me many valuable lessons for my spiritual growth. I have learned that my life holds stale things that need to be discarded and that sometimes my life feels as wounded as a broken cup. I have learned that I have flaws, chips, and stains, just as any well-used cup may have. . . . I have learned that the contents of my life are

> meant to be constantly given and shared.... I have especially learned gratitude for all those moments when the unexpected has transformed my life into an abundant cup of blessings.

Many faith paths use the bowl for spiritual meditations and prayers; the best-known practitioners of this tradition are Native Americans. In volume 4 of *The North American Indian,* Edward S. Curtis—the early twentieth-century descriptive researcher and journalist—wrote about the Ceremony of the Bowl:

> Then she revealed to him the rites of Taking Up the Bowl.
>
> A man who desires this ceremony performed climbed to the top of his earthen lodge and appealed to Old Woman Who Never Dies: "Bowl, I cause you to be taken up, that my children may grow strong. Let the rain come upon us." Or he might go to the hills and utter this prayer, crying like a child. Already he had provided offerings, and food, robes, and clothing.
>
> When all was ready he sought the Keeper of the Bowl, and offered him the pipe, apprising him of the object of his visit. The Keeper told him that he was doing right to take up the bowl, and accepted the pipe, lighted it, and prayed to the sacred vessel, which was kept in the honor place of his lodge: "Bowl, we are about to take you up again with prayers and fasting. Open your ears that you may hear our songs. Give us your aid."

Today, when using prayer bowls, Native Americans in the Zuni tribe place cornmeal inside the bowls; small stone carvings of animals, called fetishes, often are nested within for safekeeping, as they represent animal spirits that guide their users. These bowls are ceremonial; sometimes dragonflies are used as part of the design, as they are considered the carriers of prayers. The Huichol Indians in Mexico also make prayer bowls; carved from dried gourds, the bowls have colorful glass beads pressed into patterns on a layer of beeswax, which acts as an adhesive.

In the Tibetan Buddhist tradition, there are two uses for this vessel. Tibetan singing bowls are hand-cast out of metal, and "sing" when they are struck or when a stick is rubbed with some pressure along the outer rim. These are used to signal the beginning or end of a ritual or meditation, or to reaffirm a prayer. Tibetans also use offering bowls, placed on home altars and filled with water, rice, incense, shells, and flowers, offerings that symbolize purification of the senses. A related Tibetan practice is found in the Wealth Treasure Vase ceremony, done in response to a prayer petition made by the person who is to own the vase. During this ceremony, monks decorate the vases with paints and then fill them with prayers, herbs, and other blessings that will bring the owners prosperity, well-being, and the answers to their prayers.

Prayer cups, or chalices, have their origins with the Greeks and Romans, who are said to have put them on their altars. The famed Holy Grail is said to be a chalice, "the cup of thanksgiving" (1 Corinthians 10:16) used to contain the Eucharist wine. The stuff of which medieval literature (and

Indiana Jones movies) is made of, the Holy Grail was considered to be the ultimate power tool—one that makes miracles occur. Today, the symbol of the chalice is still powerful enough that in the Catholic Church, the cup holding the wine must be made of either gold or silver (and, if made of silver, then must be gilded) and consecrated by a bishop. Accordingly, this consecration is threatened if the chalice breaks or the gilt needs to be reapplied.

And the cup, to which has been added a flame, shows up as the Unitarian Universalists' denominational symbol. Yet, in true Unitarian form, according to the Unitarian Universalist Association, "No one meaning or interpretation is official. The flaming chalice, like our faith, stands open to receive new truths that pass the tests of reason, justice, and compassion."

As it has with other prayer practices, the Internet is enlivening the practice of using a prayer bowl. Internet versions of prayer bowls are mimicking those used in places of worship, into which prayer requests are made and then prayed over by volunteers or religious representatives.

There are many different forms of the prayer bowl or chalice, just as there are varied religious and cultural approaches to using it. No matter how people proceed, perhaps they will find, as did American writer and philosopher Ralph Waldo Emerson, that they "never lose an opportunity of seeing anything that is beautiful; for beauty is God's handwriting—a wayside sacrament. Welcome it in every fair face, in every fair sky, in every fair flower, and thank God for it as a cup of blessing."

Suggestions for Beginning the Exploration

- Is there a bowl or cup that has meaning for you? Begin to think of it as a spiritual tool and integrate it into your prayer time.
- If you are working with a bowl, you might place your prayers in the bowl after writing them down. If you are working with a cup or chalice, you can begin to explore its metaphorical possibilities for mirroring your life. What does working with the shape of an open vessel bring up for you spiritually?

Prayer Dancing

Worship of the One Who Created Our Bodies and Our Souls

Our lives are a dance, and our friends and families are our dancing partners, and God is the head of the dance. He calls the tunes, and directs the music, and invites us all to dance. Sometimes He even interrupts our normal dances so that He can dance just with us. . . .

—Andrew Greeley

If, as some have suggested, laughter is the universal language, then dance might well be the universal prayer. Dancing as worship is an ancient rite, practiced by every culture in the world. Sacred dance is believed to have originated in Greek temples; it was also a part of early Egyptian rituals, and the Old Testament refers to dance as worship, for example, when it teaches, "Let them praise his name with dancing, and make music to him with tambourine and harp" (Psalm 149:3). During the infancy of Christianity, the devout danced; however, dance's connection to earth-based religions later caused church officials to revoke this practice, and even today, there are Christian churches averse to liturgical dance.

Yet, as dancer Gabrielle Roth writes in her book *Sweat Your Prayers,* "The tradition of dancing into ecstasy may have been burned at the stake, but its spirit is rising from those same ashes like a Phoenix."

While we in the West are enjoying the resurgence of interest in sacred dance to which Roth refers, dance has remained a constant in many Eastern cultures. In India, dances are associated with spirituality; the movements of dance represent the rhythm of the cosmos. Indeed, the Hindu god Shiva is a dancing god, who through his dance releases souls from illusion. Farther east, there are Buddhist Dance Dramas; and even the traditional form of Japanese theater, Kabuki, is said to have been launched in the 1600s by a shrine maiden.

The dances of indigenous peoples are sometimes associated with prayers of supplication, often for rain or successful harvests and hunts. The Sioux Sun Dance—held each year during the days of the full moon in June, July, or August—is held as a thanksgiving celebration to the Great Spirit. And Sufi dancing, with its immediate association with the whirling dervishes, looks like simple folk dancing, but in it participants can travel to ecstatic heights. Dance is a form of worship that can symbolize all of human experience and cause the dancers to feel connected with the entire web of life. The famous thirteenth-century Sufi poet Rumi helps us to see dance as a prayer practice when he wrote:

> Dance, when you're broken open.
> Dance, if you've torn the bandage off.
> Dance in the middle of the fighting.

Dance in your blood.
Dance, when you're perfectly free.

There is a physiological consequence to those forms of movement we call "trance dance"—it can literally alter brainwaves, moving them into alpha and even theta states. This conduit to altered consciousness is used by shamans, who sometimes dance to effect healings in the viewers. The repetition of rhythmic, physical movement becomes a method of honing the dancer's consciousness, even allowing for communion with the Divine.

Practitioners of sacred dance use a mystical language; most express the feeling that they are not dancing the dance, but that they are *being danced* by the dance; that it is the Divine who is choreographing their steps. Having a clear intention for the dance is important to those who see it either as a prayer practice or as a ministry; they stress that it can't be about technique, about how one looks while doing it, but must simply be about glorifying the God of one's own understanding. As with other prayer practices, the object is to move the ego out of the way in order to be a vessel for Spirit. And, when it is done in the presence of others, both the dancer and the audience can receive the spiritual messages of the dance.

American choreographer and dancer Ruth St. Denis could perhaps be called the mother of contemporary sacred dance in the West. Around the turn of the twentieth century, she began performing innovative dances that were inspired by the creative and spiritual traditions of Asia, India, and Egypt. She believed that dance should promote the spiritual rather than simply entertain, and she founded the Society of Spiritual Arts. For the rest of her life—she died in 1968—she explored the possibilities of sacred dance. She was the inspiration for the founding of the Sacred Dance Guild and other organizations devoted to prayer dancing; thus her vision remains alive today. As St. Denis explained it, "My concept of the new forms of worship that would include rhythmic movement in the church services asks for no lessening of the natural dignity and solemn beauty of spiritual realization. But I call for a new, vital expression that will bring humanity into a closer, more harmonious relationship with the One who created our bodies as well as our souls."

Named by her parents for a goddess, Athena Katsaros' interest in sacred dance began when she was just a young girl and witnessed that "vital expression" that St. Denis espoused. Athena, an artist and consultant, has been dancing for almost three decades, having become captivated by dance when she was just fourteen and saw her first belly-dancing performance. "I was intrigued by the exoticism of it," she remembers. "It was flowing and feminine; there was something mystical about it." She has been belly dancing ever since—and has been teaching it, as well as other forms of expressive dance, since she was sixteen.

For Athena, dancing "became a prayer practice for me when I could feel the innate spiritual quality of the dance coming through." It became a conscious practice for her when she was in her thirties, and now prayer informs her dancing not only during it, but also beforehand. "When I perform, I ask to be a vehicle for Spirit to move through me,"

Athena says. "I always set an intention for the dance; it has to do with touching people. It's about love and transcendence, about people feeling uplifted by the experience. And, since I do Middle Eastern dance, it's also about peace. I pray to open hearts and inspire love."

Athena clearly recalls the first time that she had a transcendent experience through dance: "I was at a dance camp; there were 250 people from around the world, both musicians and dancers. One night I was chosen to dance, accompanied by world-class musicians. I came out to perform, and it was the first time I literally felt as if the music was pouring through me. I felt that I wasn't creating the dance, but that the music was moving through me and expressing itself through my body. It was as if the music was pouring into me through the top of my head like liquid. I felt it was flowing into me and out of me, and that the music itself was Spirit. I felt no separation from the music, the musicians, the audience, the Divine.

"It's an ecstatic practice," Athena explains. "My prayer practice is through dance and its connection to music. It's my way of having union with the Divine."

Suggestions for Beginning the Exploration

- Think back through any dance performances you have seen, whether they were labeled as liturgical or not. Note to yourself if you ever saw or felt Spirit as you watched someone dance.
- In your own experience of dancing, have you ever felt a shift in consciousness as a result of the movement? Has dancing ever brought you in touch with deep emotions? As an experiment, try dancing the next time you feel emotionally charged: create a dance for sadness, for anger, for joy.
- During the privacy of your quiet time, explore dancing as a form of prayer. Notice if you feel more connected to God as you dance.

PRAYER FLAGS

Carrying Blessings High and Far

The wings of prayer carry high and far.

—ANONYMOUS

Though we in the West usually associate flags with national pride, for thousands of years, the Tibetans have been using flags for quite a different purpose: prayer. For the Tibetans, these flags blow prayers for happiness, prosperity, and long life to all people in the path of the wind that has borne the blessings from the flag.

Colorful and highly decorated, covered with mantras and prayers written in Tibetan as well as representations that symbolize characteristics of the enlightened mind, prayer flags are hung both inside and outside. Everything about a prayer flag is highly symbolic, from the colors used for them to the illustrations depicted on them. Even the wind that blows them is said to symbolize the nature of our consciousness. There are horizontal prayer flags *(lung ta)* and vertical prayer flags *(dar cho)*. Horizontal flags are connected by a long cord, which is strung through the top of the individual pieces; vertical flags are either individual pieces or are sewn together, and are sometimes affixed to a large pole.

Prayer flags come in sets of five, which should be hung in the proper order—yellow, green, red, white, blue—from bottom to top, or from left to right. These colors represent the elements: earth (yellow), water (green), fire (red), cloud (white), and sky (blue). Additional symbols often printed on prayer flags with hand-carved woodblocks include four animals, each representing a particular quality. The dragon symbolizes gentle power; the snow lion, fearless joy; the tiger, confidence; and the *garuda*, a mythical bird, represents wisdom. It is believed that the image itself will invoke the qualities of that which is symbolized. Other images include the "wind horse," which has three flaming jewels on its back, symbolizing the Buddha, Buddhist teachings, and the Buddhist community.

The practice of prayer flags has its origins in Bon, Tibet's indigenous religion before Buddhism. A 1990 issue of *Me-Long*, the newsletter of the Council for Religious and Cultural Affairs of His Holiness the Dalai Lama, reported that the impetus for prayer flags can be "traced to a collection of Bonpo teachings, which say that when a mantra is wrapped in five-colored silk and placed high in the mountains, it will provide whoever sees it with the good fortune to become enlightened."

Though this suggests that prayer flags originally were hung in rural locations, Tibetans—and those they have influenced—now place prayer flags both inside and outside of their homes and places of worship. The name *lung ta,* meaning "wind horse," refers to their belief that the blessings inherent in the use of the prayer flags will be carried by the wind to all those who are in the area.

Because the prayer flags are made of cotton, when they are placed outside their colors will fade, eventually disappearing, and the flags will begin to deteriorate. For that reason, new flags supplement older flags, usually on each Tibetan New Year, in a visual acknowledgment of the cycles of birth, maturity, and death that all living things experience. Some users of the prayer flag also point to the symbolic possibilities intrinsic to the life span of the cloth; that as it ages and begins to decompose, tiny pieces of it may be ingested by birds or animals, who in turn may be eaten by us. Thus, a prayer flag may not only bring nearby beings blessings on the wind, but may actually become a part of us all.

Though there is a certain simplicity to this prayer practice, it has its own set of considerations. It is believed that putting prayer flags up on an inauspicious astrological date will bring bad luck to the user. According to Tibetan teacher Lama Zopa Rinpoche, there are antidotes you can use to avoid obstacles, such as putting any material made of iron in the east; putting water in the south; putting fire—lighted incense or matches—in the west; putting earth—sand or dirt in a container—in the north; and putting a bundle of various plants in each corner. Each direction has a specific mantra to use with the specified corrective element. But do your homework—even if you hang your prayer flags on a proper date, you'll need to take into account the difference between the Tibetan calendar and the Western calendar. Also, if you're hanging a prayer flag inside, the wall that the prayer flag is displayed on must face east or north.

A number of innovative interpretations of the prayer flag have been created, one of the most notable being as an instrument—and symbol—of healing. Though most people are probably familiar with the pictures of prayer flags that have been left at the top of Mt. Everest, that practice has been given new life. In 1995, breast cancer survivors went to Mt. Aconcagua and carried 170 prayer flags with more than 400 names inscribed on them; they followed this feat with a trip to Mt. McKinley in Alaska in 1998 and Mt. Fuji in Japan in 2000. And adapting a tradition from the Tibetans themselves, prayer flags are being incorporated into marriage ceremonies and funerals; when someone is ill, they are flown to bring health, well-being, and peace.

Whether there is a specific intention for prayer flags or not, simply seeing them can remind people to say a prayer or to be mindful as they continue with the tasks of their everyday lives. Prayer flags can gently wave into our own awareness the many colorful blessings of our lives.

Suggestions for Beginning the Exploration

- If you were to make a prayer flag, what would make it significant to you? What colors, symbols, prayers would you include on it? How would you use it? If you feel so inspired after this reflection, create your own prayer flag and incorporate it into your spiritual practice.

Prayer Rugs

A Place to Face the Gateway of Paradise

For those who have come to know God,
the whole world is a prayer mat.

—Bawa Muhaiyaddeen

For those who do not use a prayer rug or mat—called *sajjada* in Arabic—as part of their practice, it might seem like an exotic act, perhaps conjuring images of magic carpets. But for the millions of Muslims who use them, prayer rugs have a very grounded application.

Although there is some historical evidence that prayer rugs preceded Islam and were woven by Armenians before Islam's advent in the seventh century, they are now integrally associated with Muslim worshipers. While Mohammed taught that Muslims can pray anywhere, it is stipulated that the place in which one prays must be clean. For that reason, one must remove his or her shoes when entering a mosque.

The use of prayer rugs evolved from that Islamic law to ensure that the site of prayer would be completely undefiled by dirt of any sort. (This mindfulness is maintained even during the making of prayer rugs, which are often woven top-down so the weaver won't need to sit on it during its creation.) In addition, because a prostrating posture is the primary form of prayer—indeed, the word *mosque* means a "place of prostration"—forehead, hands, knees, and feet will touch the ground, which is another reason the mosque must be kept clean.

Though there are no specific dimensions given for prayer rugs, they are carried by Muslims when traveling and thus should be portable. Because people usually pray within a community, some prayer mats are big enough for two or more people praying in a row while at home. What is stressed as important is not the form, but the function—one theoretically can pray on any clean surface that covers the floor.

Muslims are required to pray five times a day; this practice is known as the *salat*. At these times, the devout need to be facing Mecca—which, depending on where the person is, sometimes is to the east, and sometimes not. To help with determining the right direction, some prayer rugs have compasses attached. Very often on a prayer rug there is an arch depicted, which represents the *mihrab,* or "gateway to paradise," in a mosque. This provides the proper direction of prayer; if you're facing the mihrab, you're facing Mecca.

Additional images sometimes included on prayer rugs are outlines of hands or feet, which show the person the correct posture for prayer; a comb or a water pitcher, which emphasizes the need for cleanliness; or a lamp, which symbolizes Allah's light. What one will never find on a prayer rug—or any Islamic art, for that matter—is a representational image of an animal or a human. These are not allowed, as it is believed that only Allah can create life. Similarly, prayer rugs will always contain some flaw or slight imperfection to represent the flaws and imperfections of humans—only Allah is perfect.

When it is the appointed time to pray, Muslims unroll their prayer rugs. They begin at dawn, then pray at noon, in the afternoon, at sunset, and at night. Though there might seem something rote about the rigorous schedule, prayer is always begun with setting the intention—praying for sincerity. Additionally, personal prayers may be added to the prescribed prayer format.

Despite its mechanics, the rewards of this prayer practice are sweet. In Coleman Barks' and Michael Green's *The Illuminated Prayer,* they portray, in text and illustration, the emotion behind the practice: "There is no single word in English that conveys the scope of the Arabic word Salat. 'Prayer,' 'blessings,' 'supplication,' and 'grace' are implied, but all fail to convey the Salat's marvelous integration of devotional heart-surrender with physical motion. In Salat, our entire being is engaged in a single luminous event."

Suggestions for Beginning the Exploration

- Note if there is a form of sacred space that you instinctively draw around your prayer life: Do you always pray by an altar, or by your bed, or in a particular chair? If not, create one. Explore how having a set place or time for your prayers affects your spiritual experience.
- Try incorporating physical movement—such as prostration—into your prayer. Notice how these actions affect your experience of the Sacred.

Prayer Wheels

Blessings and Well-Being with Every Turn

Just touching and turning a prayer wheel brings incredible purification and accumulates unbelievable merit. . . .

—Lama Zopa Rinpoche

Similar in size to a rattle, this small, hand-held device is made of copper, inlaid with turquoise and coral, with exotic brass calligraphy that spells out a prayer. It has a handle with alternating strips of brass and copper, and in the middle of its head—the part that spins—there is a tiny chain with a small weight attached that aids its rhythmic movement. Called a "prayer wheel" or "Mani wheel," this small instrument has great power: With every turn, blessings and well-being are spread to all who are nearby and continue on into the world.

Tibetans have used prayer wheels for more than a thousand years; the earliest account of their use was written in 400 C.E. by a Chinese traveler who saw prayer wheels being used when he journeyed to Ladakh. In addition to the smaller ones, which are often spun with the right hand while holding a *mala* in one's left, there are much larger prayer wheels, which are spun as one passes them, found along the walls of monasteries and shrines. One can also find tiny prayer wheels, spun on a flat surface with just two fingers.

The origin of the prayer wheel is believed to have stemmed from the phrase "turn the wheel of the dharma," which is the teaching of the Buddha. Prayer wheels are also called the "Wheel of the Law." It is believed that using the prayer wheel will reduce the amount of negative karma that the practitioner will need to work through; that when we spin the wheel, Buddhas and bodhisattvas—particularly Chenrezi, the embodiment of compassion—purify karma and help us to move further along the path to enlightenment. The prayer wheel is always spun clockwise, for not only does this acknowledge the direction of the sun and echo the path of those who circumambulate stupas—Buddhist monuments that sometimes contain relics—but it is the same order in which a reader would see the words of the prayers inside the wheel.

For that is the power of the prayer wheel: contained around its axle are rolls of thin paper on which, in ancient script, are printed prayers or mantras, primarily *"Om Mani Padme Hum"* ("Om! The jewel in the lotus of the heart"). This prayer usually adorns the outside of the prayer wheel as well, carved or applied decoratively to the top or sides. The number of prayers contained within accelerates the spiritual progress of the user; each time the prayer wheel is spun, it is equivalent to having said the prayer once—though some say that each turn is thought to be the equivalent of having said the prayer as many times as it is written inside the cylinder.

In addition to bringing spiritual rewards to the practitioner, the prayer wheel also spins those same blessings outward into the world. Thus, for many Tibetans, the prayer wheel is used when taking meditative walks. It is believed that using a prayer wheel helps to unify the practitioner's mind, body, and speech, as well as creating "merit"—a moral deposit into one's spiritual bank account, to use a metaphor, which will positively affect one's present or future life, as well as benefiting all living beings and the environment itself.

For that reason, prayer wheels are often placed where water or wind will spin them; there are also prayer wheels that are turned by flame or light. It is said that all in the vicinity of a prayer wheel will be saved from being reborn in the lower realms. In an essay written by the Tibetan teacher Lama Zopa Rinpoche, he instructs that prayer wheels can help to make environments peaceful and serene, and are also helpful for healing. Indeed, some practitioners of the prayer wheel advise using it with sick pets or with people who are dying; for the dying, it becomes a tool for transferring their consciousness from this earthly realm to the next.

As the Tibetan influence has spread throughout the world, so has the use of the prayer wheel. Prayer wheels now are being found in surprising environments, ranging from jewelry stores (you can buy tiny prayer wheels designed to be worn as pendants or earrings) to the Internet. There are a number of Web sites from which you can download computerized prayer wheels that will move on their own. A technological heresy? Not according to His Holiness the Dalai Lama, who blessed their use by saying that the electronic prayer wheel works just the same as a traditional one.

Suggestions for Beginning the Exploration

- In the Tibetan Buddhist tradition, it is considered essential to always "dedicate the merit." Reflect on who or what you would dedicate the merit to, if you were to use a prayer wheel.
- Notice what prayers or mantras are most meaningful to you. If you were to offer blessings to all those in your path, what would they be?

PRAYER WITH OTHERS

Uniting Oneself with the Community

In prayer a man should always unite himself with the community.

—THE TALMUD

Praying with others is an ancient prayer practice, as old as the tradition of gathering in a community to worship—and its value is high. According to Mohammad, "Rewards for prayers said by people assembled together are twice those said at home."

Jesus reiterated this concept when he promised that "for where two or three come together in my name, there am I with them." (However, it should be noted that some Christians disavow public prayer, pointing to Matthew 6:5-6—"And when you pray, do not be like the hypocrites, for they love to pray standing in the synagogues and on the street corners to be seen of men.... But when you pray, go into your room, close the door and pray to your Father.... "—as evidence that one should only pray in private.)

Yet for many people, on every faith path, being in fellowship with others as they worship can be a deeply moving way to pray. In addition to the immediate experience of hearing others say or whisper their prayers at the same time you do, knowing that the litany you recite has been prayerfully repeated by fellow worshipers through the centuries can help you feel connected in the great chain of belonging.

Praying in community can also deepen the prayer experience because of the interactive nature of the practice, particularly one that asks for a verbal reply, such as the "call and response" format. Saying prayers en masse has been used for hundreds of years during political or civic events, such as nonviolent civil rights protests, to cement feelings of solidarity and common purpose. Since 1952, a World Invocation Day has been held to affirm "the oneness of humanity, the livingness of our relationship to God, and the responsibility of humanity for the working out of the Divine plan on earth."

But community prayer does not have to be confined to the parameters of a worship service or public event; many prayer groups are working with the written word to garner communal prayers. For example, the United Bible Societies (USB), formed in 1946, is an international service organization that helps to coordinate the translation and production of Bibles around the world. They have a pamphlet that highlights work that is being done in particular countries, and the entries focus on a number of those places every week, thereby encouraging people to pray collectively about the issues in those countries during that time.

This example is just one of many examples of how public prayer vehicles are proliferating. According to a 1996 article in *USA Today,* "Around the nation, praying for others has become one of the hottest forms of religious outreach in the '90s." A burgeoning number of new groups are forming, called "prayer warriors," who pray for others who request it. Prayer requests are being received on paper, over toll-free telephone lines, and in Internet prayer boxes. And this is not just an American phenomenon—two Jesuits in Dublin created a Web site (*www.sacredspace.ie*) that has gotten up to one hit every thirty seconds, or 4,000 hits per day from people all over the world. The site features daily prayers that take ten minutes or so to go through, depending on how much time one wants to take to link to the additional readings, exercises, and visuals that are included to deepen the visitor's experience.

The Internet has made such an impact on prayer that some people are even calling themselves "Internet missionaries"; one Web site—*eprayer.org*—calls its focus "digital discipleship." Because of their very nature, these Internet prayer chains enable more participation in prayer. The authors of one site explain, "By sending a request to one person, you virtually have an army of people praying for you and with you. This is the concept of the 'prayer chain.'" However, like other issues that have surfaced with the Internet, some initial bugs had to be worked out: Since online prayer requests can literally be accessed by millions around the world, confidentiality should be kept in mind, both in making and responding to a prayer request.

The Vietnamese Buddhist monk and author Thich Nhat Hanh has counseled that we must "learn to look with *sangha* [community] eyes," and public prayer does foster a sense of responsibility for the common good, incorporating the communal as well as the individual. A new trend has emerged in which Web sites promote praying on particular days, at a specific time—calls for prayer have included meditations for the 2000 U.S. presidential election; "LightShift 2000," held at midnight on January 1, 2001; and a number of Middle East prayer vigils. One of them sprouted as a direct result of a comment made by a political leader—when Yasser Arafat said that peace will not come to the Middle East without a million strong prayers. In response, *emissaryoflight.com* was created in 2000 with the goal of presenting one million prayers of peace to Palestinian president Arafat and then-Israeli president Ehud Barak.

For those who remain unsure of the reason for praying with others, author Doreen Virtue, who is a leading participant in a number of the Internet calls to prayer, elucidates her viewpoint in her book *The Lightworker's Way.* Writes Virtue, "We must remember the Law of Cause and Effect: *Whatever we think about enlarges.* We who are lightworkers must daily meditate upon what we want to see, not upon what we fear may happen. . . . Your prayers, combined with those of other lightworkers, could restore the earth to her natural state of perfect, radiant health."

Suggestions for Beginning the Exploration

- Many people have had the experience of a chain of people praying for them or a family member—or have been a part of a collective that was praying for another. If you haven't, investigate ways to do so—and notice how your spiritual experience is affected by being linked in community.
- What issues or concerns—such as hunger, domestic violence, or world peace—compel you the most passionately? If you haven't done so already, research local or Internet-based groups devoted to prayer partnering and add your prayers to theirs. Reflect on how this affects your commitment to the cause.

Rituals

Relating the Physical to Higher Worlds

In the world of ritual today we find Zen Buddhist masters, mystical rabbis, Christian priests who embrace all the world's wisdom, African shamans, artists, healers, Taoist storytellers, and people who simply want to dance and sing with joy. The actual rituals themselves take the teachings out of the realm of theory and into physical and emotional reality.

—Rachel Pollack

We all have rituals, though we may be more familiar with them as family traditions or customs: always serving a particular meal on a birthday, playing certain musical pieces during the holidays, lighting a candle before one prays. A ritual can be as simple as enjoying a cup of coffee in silence before the sun comes up or creating a lengthy observance with colorful costumes and sacred objects; what makes something a ritual is the intention with which you perform it and the meaning it holds for you.

According to Z'ev ben Shimon Halevi, author of *School of Kabbalah*, "The essence of ritual is that something done in the physical realm is related to the higher worlds. This may be a simple gesture of the hand or an elaborate ceremony. It can be working consciously in everyday life, so that quite mundane actions become full of meaning, or a carefully designed ritual acted out for a specific occasion. . . . Ritual is the mode of formalizing action and giving it not only meaning, but creating a contact with other worlds."

As this passage suggests, ritual, when used as a prayer practice, can infuse our daily lives with a sense of the sacred. Through ritual we can honor the major transitions and transformations of our lives, either consciously carving meaning out of the experiences that wound us or celebrating the exhilaration of our deepest joys. Ritual, even in its simplest form, can also serve to enhance—and give us a container for—our relationship with the Divine. In *Why Christianity Must Change or Die: A Bishop Speaks to Believers in Exile,* John Shelby Spong describes how he transformed the ritual of keeping track of time: "I once even printed a cross on my watch face so that every time I glanced to establish the time of day I would be reminded to send a prayer darting heavenward to keep me connected with the God whom I hoped might be an external compass point by which my life would be guided."

Some people who have fallen away from their own faith paths because the rituals of that religion seemed too rote have found new meaning by creating their own forms of worship. Others, who don't want to be part of a formal religious tradition, also find meaning in creating ceremonies to celebrate the sacred. Cultural practices are being redefined through ritual, including forms of body art. *Mehndi,* the art of applying henna in intricate patterns on the hands and feet of women who are being married, is a beautiful ritual that has traveled from India to the Western world; and following a cue from Tahitians and other cultures, many people are getting tattoos or parts of their bodies pierced to mark important life passages.

In their book, *The Art of Ritual,* Renee Beck and Sydney Barbara Metrick recommend ten guidelines for creating your own rituals:

1. Remember the intention;
2. Let the myth inspire you;
3. Use your intuition;
4. Ensure that the ritual benefit all and harm none;
5. Keep it simple;
6. Stay balanced;
7. Keep in touch with your feelings and with other people;
8. Honor the power of words;
9. Keep the imagination alive;
10. Attend to detail.

The most important consideration when planning a ritual is also the most basic: First decide why you are performing a ritual—what your intention is—and what you desire from it. From there, decide who will be participating, what you will use in your ritual, where you will hold your ritual (by a mountain, an ocean, in the woods; facing a particular direction) and when you will perform your ritual (consider solstices and equinoxes, phases of the moon).

Once you're clear about your intention, you can begin the preparation phase. It can be very gratifying to engage all of the physical senses, so think of elements you can incorporate that will appeal to your sense of touch, taste, smell, sound, and sight. Don't forget the importance of movement in your ritual, and explore the possibilities of color. And remember that anything that has significance for you can become part of the ceremony.

Having at least a cursory awareness of symbology—knowing what particular numbers, colors, and objects represent in folklore, as well as what they represent to you—can enhance your ritual. Objects used in your ritual can include candles, herbs, salt, incense, oils, feathers, shells, stones, flowers, and ribbons. You can begin by purifying your ritual space and yourself with an element such as sage or lavender; then invoke the Divine presence to be with you as you express your thanks.

Remember that there are no rights and wrongs in ritual; what is important is your sacred intention. No matter how much you plan your ritual, you will probably re-enter the world having been changed. Though we perform rituals to celebrate our transformations, the act of doing a ritual itself can transform us. Because of its intensity, it needs to have a beginning, a middle, and a clearly defined conclusion.

This is a concept that Ann Keeler Evans, a former business consultant turned ecumenical minister and theologian, knows intimately. She even started her business, A Rite to Remember, to contribute ritual to the important ceremonies of people's lives. Says Ann, "Ritual has purpose—even if it's just to open yourself. It's a lot like a factory: You come in with an idea of something and the raw goods to make it, and in the process, something else mooshes out at the other end."

Ann stresses the importance of doing ritual in community; though she acknowledges that it can be done alone, she thinks the experience is not as rich. "You can do ritual on your own, but I think it misses the mark. A strengthening piece of ritual is witness. And in some ways the other pieces may just be ritual action—setting up your altar, doing certain things on holidays—but having the shared vision of that deepens the ritual."

Ann continues, "I think ritual makes a difference in the way we live our lives—it assists in clarifying our intentions. It deepens the possibilities for getting what we want." But for Ann, ritual is not a formula for some kind of cosmic gumball machine; it is a prayer practice. As she explains, "Ritual is prayer because it's time for taking time apart—time outside of time, place outside of place—to be involved in meaning with others, in making and understanding meaning and allowing that to reflect in our lives. It is a form of prayer that is not without history, and as such it needs to be taken very seriously, because it can and will change your life."

Suggestions for Beginning the Exploration

- Think back to the events of your life that were marked in some special way—perhaps as simply as with a congratulatory dinner out, a surprise bouquet of flowers, or with a handwritten card or letter. Did having this kind of ceremonial acknowledgment deepen those experiences?
- What customs or traditions do you currently practice now? Investigate ways you could deepen those experiences by being even more mindful about the way you approach them.
- Explore bringing more ceremony or ritual into your prayer life, outside of your place of worship. Note how this affects your relationship with God.

SACRED SCRIPTURES

Reading That Feeds the Soul

Let no day pass by without reading some portion of the Sacred Scriptures and giving some space to meditation; for nothing feeds the soul so well as those sacred studies do.

—THEONAS OF ALEXANDRA

Reading sacred scriptures is considered an activity so edifying that in the Catholic Church, a person can receive a partial indulgence if he or she does a spiritual reading from sacred scripture; if the reading continues for a half-hour or more, a plenary indulgence—formally defined as "the remission before God of the temporal punishment due to sins, already forgiven as far as the sin is concerned"—is granted. But the age-old prayer practice of reading sacred texts is not only a foundation of the Christian church, but of every major faith tradition of the world. Given the wide adoption and acceptance of scripture, it might seem as if there is nothing fresh to explore. But many people are discovering what for them are innovative ways of encountering holy words, and their spiritual lives are being enriched from their new approaches.

According to Islamic teachings, "The Koran was sent down in seven dialects, and in every one of its sentences there is an outer and an inner meaning." Given this, the subject of reading scriptures has compelled many theologians to offer their opinions on the best way to go about it. In his work *On First Principles,* a third-century Christian writer named Origen elucidated his belief that scripture speaks to people on different levels, according to their maturity and perception: "Divine things are communicated to men somewhat obscurely and are the more hidden in proportion to the unbelief or unworthiness of the inquirer."

For Origen, the first level of understanding was literal interpretation—a plane of comprehension that still informs many believers today. Moving past that, Origen wrote, is the second level, where one encounters the spirit of the scripture. The third level is the spiritual dimension, where those who read are actually inspired by the words to live holy lives. Augustine would seem to agree with this delineation; in his *Confessions,* he wrote, "There are others for whom the words of Scripture are no longer a nest but a leafy orchard, where they see the hidden fruit. They fly about it in joy, breaking into song as they gaze at the fruit and feed upon it."

Thus, when endeavoring to enliven this prayer practice in one's own life, it helps to see the different possibilities for scripture: as story, as metaphor, as inspiration. Furthermore, there are the actions one takes to explore these different possibilities. In his *Letter on the Contemplative Life,* Guigo II, a Cistercian prior at Chartres during the twelfth century, wrote this: "Reading seeks the sweetness of the blessed life, while meditation finds it. Prayer asks for it and contemplation tastes it. Reading, in a certain way, brings solid food to the mouth, meditation chews and breaks it up, prayer obtains its seasoning, contemplation is the same sweetness which refreshes and brings joy."

An ancient form of contemplating sacred scriptures, rooted in the tradition of Benedictine monks, has been rediscovered and increasingly is being practiced by contemporary spiritual seekers: Lectio Divina (meaning "spiritual reading" in Latin). In Lectio Divina, practitioners encounter their reading of scripture in four parts. The first part is the *lectio,* or reading, where one asks oneself what the text actually says. Then comes the *meditatio,* or meditation, in which one asks how the text relates to him or her personally. This is followed by *oratio,* or prayer, in which the practitioner ponders what God is saying through the text, and asks God how to respond to it. The concluding part is the *actio,* or living, in which one discerns how this experience can affect the way he or she now lives life.

Another way to approach reading scriptures as a prayer practice is to do what is referred to as "imaginative reading," in which—as the name implies—one uses one's imagination to visualize the very scenes he is reading about. In his book *Imagine Jesus. . . ,* Father Frank Andersen writes, "Only in our imagination do we 'build a coherent picture' out of the many different influences on our lives: our reading and study, our reflection and prayer, our hard-won experience, and those people who affect us deeply. It's in our imagination that we 'put it all together' and make sense of things—we imagine what God is like, and we imagine what life is about."

Imagining being in the scene of the scriptural story and actually talking with the people who are depicted in it—including spiritual leaders—can strengthen one's feeling of relationship with and understanding of God. For this practice, one can use a study guide, such as Father Andersen's, or simply stay with the passage one is working with long enough to imagine what it was like to be there.

For others, a nonstructured approach may be preferred, in which one simply reads a passage slowly, then stops, to see what emerges in one's heart and mind. When one wants to interact more actively with the scriptures, a set of simple questions can be applied, such as: What is this saying? What is this symbolizing? What is this stirring within me personally? What tells me about God? What tells me about myself? What is useful to me; what can I take away from this?

These practices show that there are approaches to sacred scriptures that go beyond the simple reading of them or even study of them. As it is said in the Hindu tradition,

> Study the words, no doubt, but look
> Behind them to the thought they indicate,
> And having found it, throw the words away
> As chaff when you have sifted out the grain.

We can use our reading as a way to commune with the Divine, to use the string of words we encounter as a rope to ascend—following its trail into a higher understanding and experience of God.

Suggestions for Beginning the Exploration

- Reflect on the scriptural passages from your own faith tradition that have nourished you the most. Which of them has influenced the way you live—or see—your life? Keep a list of them in your journal.
- Try imaginative reading when you next explore a spiritual story. Notice how actively using your imagination affects your sense of yourself—and your sense of God.

SAINTS

Communing with the Sanctified or Holy Ones

The veneration in which a Tolstoy, a St. Francis, a crucified Christ, and the saints of all the ages have been held proves that, in the inner sanctuary of their souls, selfish men know that they ought not to be selfish, and venerate what they feel they ought to be. . . .

—REINHOLD NIEBUHR

Though there are saints in other religions, the word *saint* is usually associated with the Christian church, primarily its Orthodox and Catholic branches. Indeed, the approach to saints has drawn a dividing line between believers; Protestants stopped acknowledging them when Martin Luther eradicated the "cult of the saints" in the sixteenth century.

The word for saint or saints that is used in Christian scriptures is *hagios,* which translates as "sanctified" or "holy ones." In a prayer, Saint Augustine elucidates what saints are and what their relationship to us is:

> O happy saints who rejoice in God; After having passed through the tempestuous sea of this life, you have merited to arrive at the port of eternal repose and sovereign peace where, sheltered from tempests and peril, you are made partakers of endless glory and happiness. I beseech you, by the charity with which your souls are replenished, to regard us with a favorable eye. . . .
>
> You are the saints and favorites of God; plead our cause before Him with so much force and ardor, and ask him so earnestly to associate us with you, that we may one day be so happy as to bless eternally His mercies, and testify to you our gratitude forever.

As this suggests, saints are seen as being intercessors for us; because they are sanctified, their prayers, in effect, pull more weight with God than do those of mere mortals. And that's exactly where the controversy lies between the Protestant and other branches of the Christian church: whether or not we need to have a righteous "middle man" or whether our prayers are powerful enough when we pray directly to God.

In the New Testament, the word *saint* refers to all believers; the line in the Apostles Creed—"I believe in the communion of saints"—refers to any believer who is, or was, a follower of Jesus Christ. Therefore, those who are opposed to praying to saints suggest that we all are to pray to God alone, as we are all equal under the mantle of our collective belief.

Yet those who advocate praying with saints point out verses such as 1 Thessalonians 5:25, in which Paul asks, "Brothers, pray for us." The implication, they say, is that we are called upon to ask others to pray with and for us—that it is the way that we support each other. Therefore, just as we would ask a brother or sister in Christ to pray for us, we can ask for prayer support from the saints. This is the crucial point to make when discussing the practice of praying with saints: Saints are not worshiped themselves, they are not the entities to whom we are praying; we are simply asking them to pray with us. It comes down to a matter of a preposition; that saints are not so much prayed to, but prayed through.

In the Orthodox Church, there are six classifications of saints: the Apostles, the Prophets, the Martyrs, the Fathers and Hierarchs of the Church, the Monastics, and the Just. According to the Orthodox Church, "We look to [saints'] lives for strength and encouragement, and continue to pray to them to intercede on our behalf to the Lord." Because saints can not only provide intercession, but also serve as role models of faith and behavior, references to them—in the form of medals, cards, statues, and portraits—are often collected by believers to reinforce their relationship to the saint.

This idea of relationship is important, because saints are seen as being alive, albeit in the realm of Spirit. Thus, praying to saints becomes a conversation of intimacy; the saint is another supporter in one's spiritual circle, a part of one's community. Patron saints are saints who represent particular interests and are sympathetic to them; sometimes those concerns were part of the saint's own life experience. There are a number of directory-like reference books listing the causes of patron saints, ranging from the specific (Need to protect your crops from pests? Call on Saint Michael of Synnada) to the general (Encountering a difficult situation of any sort? Saint Eustace can help).

But, as Anthony M. Buono points out in "Praying with the Saints," "Possibly the most important function of the saints on our behalf . . . is their role as exemplars or models. They show us how to pray by their words and how to live by their deeds. The most powerful words they utter are the words of their prayers. . . . By praying these . . . we will undoubtedly deepen our own prayer life."

Suggestions for Beginning the Exploration

- Are there any prayers that are attributed to saints—such as Saint Francis' well-known prayer—that have inspired you to learn about that saint? If not, try reading about the saint to discover if that knowledge informs your understanding of or experience with the prayer.
- If you haven't previously explored the lives of saints, take a look at Robert Ellsberg's book *All Saints*. Formatted for daily reflection, Ellsberg provides 365 short biographies on people ranging from the apostle Saint James to South African freedom fighter Stephen Biko. Track how their examples affect your life or relationship with God.

SERVICE

The Path to Joy and Re-Creation

Through selfless service, you will always be fruitful and find fulfillment. This is the promise of the Creator.

—BHAGAVAD GITA

In the last several decades, the topic of service has been increasingly covered by the media and by politicians, and in an age of cynicism and reality TV, that's a good thing. Former President George H. Bush encouraged volunteerism by calling for a "thousand points of light," and when President Bill Clinton signed the King Holiday and Service Act in 1994, it was for the purpose of sanctioning Martin Luther King Day as a day of community service. Think about it: Haven't you seen a "Practice Random Acts of Kindness and Senseless Acts of Beauty" bumper sticker on the back of a car, or had your bridge toll paid by a charitable driver in front of you?

There is a curious paradox surrounding service, an almost reversible reaction that occurs when we subvert our natural tendencies to seek our own good and focus instead on providing good to others. Sages throughout time have taught that service, even though it involves self-sacrifice, brings its own set of rewards: As the renowned Indian poet Tagore expressed it, "I slept and dreamt that life was joy, / I awoke and saw that life was service, / I acted and behold, service was joy."

Serving others is encouraged in every major world religion. Indeed, scriptures from all faith traditions not only emphasize service, but extol it as the epitome of human achievement. In Jainism, it is taught that "rendering help to another is the function of all human beings" (*Tattvarthasutra* 5.21). And Islam teaches that service is the pinnacle of actualization: "The best of men are those who are useful to others" (Hadith of Bukhari). Confucianism sees service not as a means to an end, but as a natural outgrowth of spiritual evolution: "The man of perfect virtue, wishing to be established himself, seeks also to establish others; wishing to be enlarged himself, he seeks also to enlarge others" (*Analects* 6.28.2).

And if, as the Talmud teaches, "all men are responsible for one another" (Sanhedrin 27b), then exactly how are we to go about demonstrating this responsibility? Jesus exemplified the calling very tangibly—if not necessarily literally—in John 13:12–16: "When he had finished washing their feet, he put on his clothes and returned to his place. 'Do you understand what I have done for you?' he asked them. . . . 'Now that I, your Lord and Teacher, have washed your feet, you also should wash one another's feet.'"

A modern spiritual master, Mahatma Gandhi, would see such a simple act as every bit as vital as something done on a larger scale. He taught that "no matter how small what you do may seem, it's vitally important that you do it." Acts of service in turn give a sense of purpose to the person who is providing the service. As artist and philosopher Benjamin Crème expressed it, "Altruistic service enables one to carry out the soul's purpose in the everyday world, thereby decentralizing one's focus and enhancing spiritual growth." And this sense of purpose is very real—in fact, scientists studying the physiological ramifications of providing service have found that it results in what they call "the helper's high."

Not only has research shown that volunteering can help one's own health; service might even prolong your life. At the University of Michigan, researchers found in a 1988 study that life expectancy increases for people who volunteer—250 percent for men. And a study at Duke University suggests why; it showed that former cardiac patients who volunteered to help patients who had just been diagnosed not only improved their mood levels, but also their levels of immune system functioning.

Yet service may not be quite as simple as it seems—for in order to truly be of service, one must let go of one's own expectations for recognition, acknowledgment, any conscious or unconscious feelings of superiority or power, even one's own views about what should happen as a result of the service. Author and teacher Ram Dass, whose *How Can I Help?* focuses on the topic of service, or "compassion in action," spoke to this subject in a *Thinking Allowed* interview, noting that service is "a very precise method of enlightenment—of serving where there is no server, because the *Bhagavad Gita* says, 'Be not identified with being the actor, and be not attached to the fruits of the action.' You're not the helper, you're the help, and who's getting helped remains open to question."

In other words, service is not only about what you do, but how and why you do it—it must come from a place of integrity, gratitude, and love. As writer Oswald Chambers expressed it, "Service is the overflow which pours from a life filled with love and devotion. But strictly speaking, there is no *call* to do that. Service is what I bring to the relationship and is the reflection of my identification with the nature of God. Service becomes a natural part of my life. God brings me into the proper relationship with Himself so that I can understand His call, and then I serve Him on my own out of a motivation of absolute love."

Service is an extension of our relationship with the Divine; it flows from our experience of Spirit in private as an urge to merge with others, giving us in the process new meaning and a new sense of our interconnectedness. It is the link in the chain that can affect real change; but in order to do so, we must start at the beginning, making sure our own spiritual house is in order before attempting to clean up the larger institutions in our lives. And in the doing, we will make ourselves new again, as well; as Gandhi wrote, "God demands nothing less than complete self-surrender as the price of the only real freedom worth having. And, when we lose ourselves, we immediately find ourselves in the service of all that lives. It becomes our joy and re-creation. We are a new person, never weary of spending ourselves in the service of God's creation."

Suggestions for Beginning the Exploration

- Think about those around you—do you have an aging parent or neighbor who needs help? Write down some ideas for what you could do for them—or do more regularly—that would be of service.
- Consider giving service anonymously. List what kind or helpful acts you can do—and not be discovered.
- Do what is meaningful to you, and don't think service only comes in big packages. Think small: Mother Teresa taught that love is small things done greatly. Smiling at people on the street, holding doors open, picking up litter are all ways of being in service.

SHADOW WORK

Enlightenment through Exploring the Darkness

One does not become enlightened by imagining figures of light, but by making the darkness conscious.

—CARL GUSTAV JUNG

Of all the prayer practices that are open to us, doing shadow work—exploring those aspects of one's unconscious that one might just as soon ignore—is perhaps one of the most difficult and yet most necessary acts for deepening one's spiritual life. As writer Madeleine L'Engle points out in *Walking on Water: Reflections on Faith and Art,* there is a root relationship between the words *heal, whole,* and *holy.* We need to heal, to embrace all parts of ourselves and accept our wholeness, before we can truly live the holy life we desire. It is an ironic fact that while repressing or denying our negative tendencies may make them seem to go away, when we least expect it we will encounter them again, bigger than ever—so addressing these parts of ourselves is the core of shadow work. What we will discover in the process is Divine grace.

The term "shadow" was coined by Swiss psychologist Carl Jung; according to Jung, we go through life projecting aspects of ourselves onto others. In other words, that which we hate—or love—about others reflects aspects of ourselves that we have not yet brought into our consciousness. We see the shadow in archetypes that have been with us throughout civilization; we can be pretty certain we're walking in shadow territory when we're tempted to divide any group of people into "the good guys" and "the bad guys." Interestingly, Jung also introduced the concept of the "bright" or "golden" shadow—that we also project great admiration onto others that might be more fruitfully used to develop those same qualities in oneself.

Yet lest we be tempted to engage in projection at this point—and see the shadow as "bad"—it should be noted that the shadow is considered to bear great gifts, that often what we feel is the worst aspect of ourselves is in actuality intrinsically related to our best. Shadow work could be said to be akin to mining: If we can learn to descend, to enter the darkness and face that rocky, dusty wall, we can begin to explore the jewels embedded within.

Psychotherapist Connie Zweig is coauthor with Steve Wolf of *Romancing the Shadow,* and founder of the Institute for Shadow-Work and Spiritual Psychotherapy in Los Angeles. In an interview with *Insight & Outlook,* she explained shadow work's connection to the spiritual life: "All of those ancient spiritual traditions knew that at some point you meet the demons on the path. It was understood that meeting the shadow was an integral part of religious and spiritual teaching. . . . In our eagerness to be more spiritual, more conscious, more aware, we have lost contact with the lower worlds."

Zweig points out that in other cultures, such as the Balinese, the dark side is openly acknowledged—one even will see masks of demons hung over doorways, placed there to greet visitors.

In a culture that equates holiness with sweetness and angels, and not masks of demons, it might be hard to fully comprehend why one would want to engage in shadow work. It is a question that *A Course in Miracles* addresses: "Fail not in your function of loving in a loveless place made out of darkness and deceit, for thus are darkness and deceit undone." In other words, it is only by facing that which is darkest in us that we can begin to undo it. And the rewards for doing that are great, as Zweig pointed out in an interview in *Kindred Spirit*. By uncovering and relating to one's shadow, it will lose its power—allowing the person to "again hear the voice of the self, the voice of your own intuitive wisdom, the part of you that knows what is right action. Carl Jung used to say that if we can shed a little light on our own darkness, it will remove some of the larger darkness from the world."

Therefore, shadow work becomes a prayer practice not just so that we may more fully be in a relationship with our God, ourselves, and our world, but because by doing shadow work, we can help to ensure that our own shadows won't be running the show—at least not as often. By healing the parts of ourselves that are in shadow, we in a very real sense contribute to the healing of the world, since the shadow uses blame or dislike of other people to distract an individual from self-examination. Once we see that the qualities we see in others are aspects of ourselves, we move out of blame and judgment into a sense of responsibility, or, to use current business terms, from reaction into proactivity. Thus, by prayerfully becoming conscious of that which is in our "lower self," we can more often act out of our higher self.

Suggestions for Beginning the Exploration

- As Zweig suggests, we can best tell when we're triggered by shadow material from the reactions of our body. Begin to track when you have strong physical reactions to things, and go digging for shadow information from there.
- When you have a strong reaction, positive or negative, to someone, try personalizing your thoughts. Instead of noting how opinionated he is or how wise she is, turn it around: "I am so opinionated"; "I am so wise." Stay with the thought, and later bring it into prayer.

STORYTELLING

Words That Excite or Calm Souls

The word is total:
it cuts, excoriates
forms, modulates
perturbs, maddens
cures or directly kills
amplifies or reduces
According to intention
It excites or calms souls.

—PRAISE SONG OF A BARD OF THE BAMBARA KOMO SOCIETY

Isak Dinesen once wrote that "all suffering is bearable if it is seen as part of a story," which may be one of the reasons that every culture, every religious tradition, every group of people throughout civilization has practiced storytelling. Telling a story allows us to comfort, to acknowledge, to inspire, to heal, to remember, to teach—and to honor the Divine of our understanding. As cultural anthropologist and author Angeles Arrien points out, "Stories are about the truths within us."

Storytelling has been a method of communicating about the sacred since the beginning of humankind. From Greek myths to Indonesian shadow plays dramatizing Hindu epics, from Native American creation stories to African call-and-response community gatherings, cultures around the world have gathered together for the weaving of spiritual lessons into their stories.

One religious culture that continues to esteem storytelling is Hasidism. Hasidim believe that when hearing a story, one should infer that the story is being told for one's own benefit, even if others are present, and thus are called to reflect personally on what that story might mean.

Tales about the Hasidic saints, called *tzaddikim*, are particularly relished. A story is told about Rabbi Israel of Rizhin, who makes a compelling case for storytelling as prayer:

> The time for prayer has already passed and I didn't pray. But, essentially, what is the difference between telling stories about tzaddikim and praying? Prayer is in the category of "Praise the Lord!" while telling stories is in the category, "Praise the servants of the Lord!" In the Book of Psalms, King David sometimes puts "Praise the Lord!" before "Praise the servants of the Lord!" but other times he puts them in the reverse order, indicating that they are equal. This teaches us that telling tales of the tzaddikim is the same as praying.

Author Susan Lowell might agree, having written that "storytellers, like apostles, are fishers of men." The holy scriptures of all major faith traditions are composed of stories—through stories we understand the nature of our God and the nature of our fellow human beings. Through stories we make sense of the world, understand the behaviors and values that are expected of us, offer hope and provide empowerment, record our histories, connect with our communities, and inspire ourselves and others to greater levels of transformation.

In addition, something magical happens when we use the form of story: we tap not only into our own imaginal realms, but also into the collective unconscious. Therefore, all stories are universal; though styles of storytelling vary, we are connected by the commonality of being human in an often capricious world. Through story we make meaning; we become creators as we attempt to understand our Creator. As African writer and storyteller Chinua Achebe expressed it: "The story is our escort; without it, we are blind. Does the blind man own his escort? No, neither do we the story; rather it is the story that owns us and directs us."

And if it is the story that "owns us and directs us," then we need to be careful about the stories we tell ourselves. There are negative, as well as positive, aspects to stories, which is why stories that honor the sacred are so desperately needed today. Just as the advent of printing supplanted storytelling, so now is upgraded technology—in the form of television, movies, and computer games—increasingly taking the place of the printed word. This has the potential to harm our children, whose stories now often consist of the lowest common denominators rather than the highest. It has been reported that in a single year, an American child will view 12,000 acts of violence, 14,000 sexual references, and almost 20,000 commercials. We also are losing the stories of elders when we do not honor them. Author Alex Haley made this point most powerfully when he wrote, "The death of an old person is like the burning of a library."

Yet there are new forms of storytelling that are sprouting and can be cultivated. Some popular entertainment is proving to address ancient archetypes in innovative ways, such as the *Star Wars* series. In an interview with Bill Moyers, director George Lucas proclaimed that he is "telling an old myth in a new way." And the growth of support groups, based on the model of Alcoholics Anonymous, provides a forum for stories that teach its listeners about the depths of hell—and the found grace that can radically change lives. As author Barry Lopez writes, "The stories people tell have a way of taking care of them. If stories come to you, care for them. And learn to give them away where they are needed. Sometimes a person needs a story more than food to stay alive. That is why we put these stories in each other's memory. This is how people care for themselves."

Suggestions for Beginning the Exploration

- Sit quietly for fifteen minutes and make a list of the stories that have nourished your life. Have any of them come from a particular faith tradition?
- Think back to what has recently stirred your soul in the form of conversation, book, magazine, television program, Internet article, or movie. Consider the story that was at the heart of it all.

- Become more conscious of the stories you tell others. Look at storytelling as a prayer practice. Notice the different effects on listeners to the story of all the things that went wrong today and the story of the kind older man who gave you his place in the supermarket line.

Sweat Lodges

A Place That Gives Strength and Power

The sweat bath is one of the most essential religious observances. Through its agency their purified minds and bodies are brought in accord with the supernatural powers. Even when it is employed in healing disease the thought is that the power of the spirits, not the steam, will expel the sickness.

—Edward S. Curtis

Though sweat baths have been practiced in different forms by many peoples of the world, including inhabitants of Europe, Scandinavia, Russia, Africa, Central America, Japan, the Middle East, and the Mediterranean, the reasons for that practice have been primarily health-related. But for Native Americans, the practice of spending time in a sweat lodge—known as *Inipi*—goes far deeper. For them, it is a spiritual ceremony that offers the gifts of purification, healing, renewal, and power.

In *Legends Told by the Old People,* the story is told of how the sweat-lodge ceremony came to be: "Sweat Lodge, left alone, spoke to himself: 'All now are gone, and the new

People will be coming soon. When they arrive they should find something to give them strength and power. I will place myself on the ground, for the use of Human Beings who are to come. Whoever visits me now and then, to him I will give power. . . .'"

The practice of the sweat lodge was first recorded in the late seventeenth century. It consists of ceremoniously constructing the lodge, which is done in prayer, using elements that carry symbolic significance, such as cedar wood, which is believed to enhance prayer. The sweat lodge is built by creating a wooden domed frame that is later covered with canvas, blankets, or animal skins; a pit is dug in the center of the lodge to hold heated rocks.

A fire is built nearby, in which to heat the rocks that will later be moved to the center of the lodge. Prayer is an integral part of the ceremony throughout its duration and during its creation: Those who gather the rocks and tend the fire offer their prayers that the participants of the sweat lodge will benefit from the experience.

An altar is made outside of the sweat lodge, using the dirt that came from the hole in which the hot rocks will be placed. On it, participants place things of special significance to them, such as a feather or stone. Nearby, the door to the sweat lodge is constructed low to the ground, in order to keep the heat inside from escaping. There is a metaphorical consequence to the structural necessity: having to bow down in order to enter the sweat lodge reinforces an attitude of humility; and since one also needs to leave the lodge by crawling, the action signifies rebirth.

Because the sweat lodge is seen as a holy place, even considered by some tribes as representing the womb of Mother Earth, careful preparation must occur before entering it. Participants often fast before the ceremony and spend time in contemplation. One is usually purified with sage smoke before entering the sweat lodge; participants then sit down on the floor of the lodge, wearing a bathing suit, shorts, a towel—or nothing at all.

Once participants have entered the lodge, moving in a clockwise position, they sit in a circle around the pit. Hot rocks are brought inside the lodge; then water is poured on them to create steam. This vapor symbolizes the breath of the Divine.

The "sweat" is usually done in four rounds, each lasting approximately forty-five minutes. After a round, the fire tender brings in more heated rocks to replace the cooling ones already in the lodge. In the dark, during a round, participants pray, chant, drum; sometimes they make declarations or simply sit in silence watching the glowing red outlines of the rocks, which illustrate the radiance of Spirit.

Practitioners of the sweat lodge believe that the ceremony provides them with spiritual cleansing, that it increases their awareness and opens their hearts. A sweat-lodge ceremony is highly significant in itself, though it also is held before other important rituals, such as a vision quest. After the participants leave the lodge, they wash themselves with water to complete their cleansing. It is said that the sweat-lodge ceremony was given to men by women, who already had the ability to cleanse themselves through their monthly cycles. (Women who are menstruating can participate in a "moon lodge," a sweat-lodge ceremony held exclusively for them.)

As with other prayer practices, it is vitally important to respect the sacred tradition of the sweat lodge. Because the practice has been appropriated by people from other cultures who do not have full knowledge of the sweat lodge's spiritual significance, many Native Americans understandably feel that something holy has been stolen from them. But simply holding a "sweat" does not mean that one has truly experienced the practice of the sweat lodge. In the paraphrased words of Lakota sweat leader Bobby Woods, "All things employed in the sweat rite are holy to the Native American and must be thoroughly comprehended . . . for the true power of a thing or an act is found in the understanding."

Suggestions for Beginning the Exploration

- If you feel called to do a sweat-lodge ceremony, first focus on your intention—why do you want to do it? Since an aspect of the sweat is spiritual cleansing, begin by examining why you want cleansing and ask, in prayer, how to best move forward.
- Examine the ceremonies of your own faith tradition. Are there any that incorporate the elements of prayerful creation, community, healing, and purification? Could you create your own ceremony for those purposes?
- If, after doing the steps above, you still want to experience a sweat-lodge ceremony, start by doing an Internet search using those words. By sifting through the listings, you will begin to discover what speaks to your needs.

TAIZE PRAYER

Singing That Continues in the Silence of One's Heart

Nothing is more conducive to a communion with the living God than a meditative common prayer with . . . singing that never ends and that continues in the silence of one's heart when one is alone again. When the mystery of God becomes tangible through the simple beauty of symbols, when it is not smothered by too many words, then prayer with others, far from exuding monotony and boredom, awakens us to heaven's joy on earth.

—BROTHER ROGER SCHUTZ, FOUNDER OF TAIZE

A space illuminated by candlelight, enhanced with elements of beauty—perhaps an icon, the resonance of rhythmic chants and scriptural reading, then a deep immersion into silence—these are the components of a Taize (pronounced *tay-zay*) prayer service, in which the whole is a communal spiritual celebration greater than the sum of its parts.

The word *Taize* is the name of a village near Cluny, France, that houses a community of brothers founded by Brother Roger Schutz during World War II.

Then twenty-five years old, Brother Roger found in Taize a house for sale that he could use to shelter a Christian community as well as to protect Jews and other refugees hiding from the Nazis. The story is told that when he found the house, an old woman who lived in Taize asked him to stay there because the townspeople were so isolated. Brother Roger heard in the woman's plaintive request the voice of God speaking to him—and today the Taize community that he founded consists of approximately one hundred brothers from twenty-five countries around the world.

Simplicity is the guiding principle behind the Taize prayer service; in a conscious attempt to welcome all people to its practice, the format of the service is kept uncomplicated. Perhaps for this reason, many churches in America—of various denominations—now offer Taize prayer to their congregations. Yet the simplicity of the service allows for it to be adapted to any environment, including a person's home. The key to practitioners' spiritual experience is not the place, but the repetition of simple songs and phrases and the attendant silence. For those who practice Taize, its deliberate simplicity is a powerful tool for accessing the Divine.

Writes Taize's founder, "Extensive knowledge is not important at the outset. In time that will be of great value. But it is through the heart, in the depths of themselves, that human beings begin to grasp the Mystery of Faith. Everything is not granted at once. An inner life is developed step by step. Today, more than in the past, we enter into the faith by going forward in stages." In addition, Brother Roger writes, "Prayer expressed in song remains one of the most essential expressions of our search for God. Short chants, repeated over and over, emphasize the meditative quality of prayer. They express in a few words a basic truth which is quickly grasped by the mind and gradually penetrates in one's whole being."

Accordingly, in a Taize prayer service, one sings—often a cappella—simple chants of one or two lines; since the music is the prayer, these chants are repeated over and over. They are sometimes sung in French, Spanish, Latin, or German, and sometimes accompanied by musical instruments such as a flute or violin, but it is the very repetition of the chants that serves like a mantra to invite a meditative sense of altered—or altared—time and dimension. The service usually includes readings from the psalms and the Gospels, prayers of intercession, and a period of deep silence, lasting anywhere from ten to twenty minutes.

Much of Taize prayer partners with symbolism; the candles that light the service illustrate the light of Christ's love that is present even in a metaphorical darkness.

And the keeping of silence, precious enough as a respite from our rapidly paced worlds, is also a reminder that words are inadequate for expressing the deep desire we hold in our hearts and souls to be in the presence of God.

Pope John XXIII called Taize "the little springtime in the Church"; today, pilgrims from all over the world, of every age and background, come to the Taize community to experience its singular form of prayer. The brothers of the Taize community, who pray three times a day, are self-supporting through their own work; Brother Roger calls them to "be filled with the Spirit of the Beatitudes: joy, simplicity, and mercy."

Again, the power of symbol is also applied to the community itself, as Brother Roger wants the Taize community to be a symbol of hope—"a spirituality of celebration" and "a parable of communion, where people seek to be reconciled every day." And, as befits a tradition that was founded during the fighting of a costly world war, when entering the Church of Reconciliation at Taize, one sees a sign that reads, "Let all who enter here be reconciled, brother with brother, sister with sister, nation with nation."

Suggestions for Beginning the Exploration

- Incorporate the reading of sacred passages and the singing of chants or meditative songs into your prayer time, then allow yourself to sink into a long period of silence. How does this contribute to your spiritual experience? How would doing it in community contribute to your spiritual experience?
- Experiment with adding elements to make your prayer space beautiful—depending on your faith path, you might want to add a standing cross or other religious representation, flowers, or candles.

TANTRIC SEX

A Way to Experience Transcendent Union with God

The sexual function is the marriage of the conscious and the unconscious and also the third party, the synthesis with the Buddha of immeasurable radiance.

—JOSEPH CAMPBELL

Of all the spiritual practices, Tantric sex is perhaps the most misunderstood. The reasons for this are many; in the Judeo-Christian religious tradition, sex has hardly been celebrated as a path to the Divine. Despite Solomon's Song of Songs, historically the sexual act has been viewed as a means for procreation, not for pleasure—and certainly not as a means to experience the sacred. Another obstacle, perhaps, is that with the resurgence of interest in Tantric sex in a Western culture that is already permeated with sexual imagery, sometimes motivations for practicing this prayer form aren't of the purest, most spiritual sort. But for those who have studied its intricacies and understand its disciplines, Tantric sex offers a way to experience nothing less than transcendent union with God.

The practice originated in India in 3000 B.C.E., although sexuality as a sacred practice also has a history in Tibet, China, the Middle East, and Europe. Incorporating ritual, yoga, and meditation, Tantric sex is seen as a method for experiencing the Divine. The word *tantra* has its roots in ancient Sanskrit and means "to weave or extend"—which refers to becoming physically and spiritually woven not only with your partner, but to all living things. Practitioners of Tantric sex point to heightened feelings of interconnectedness, mystical union, and oneness with all—including God—as the fruits of this endeavor.

The foundation of the Tantric tradition are the Hindu gods Shakti and Shiva, who represent the female and male principles. The union of this goddess and god resulted in the universe's very creation, and represents its perfect balance and harmony through this pairing of female and male—yin and yang—energy. This sense of harmony is what many practitioners of Tantric sex point to as being of benefit—a feeling of well-being that not only affects the couple but reverberates out into the world.

Though Tantra was practiced in India for hundreds of years before being adopted into the Buddhist tradition, it is in Tibet that the Tantric tradition is said to have achieved its highest levels of practice. But devoted practitioners note that sex is not the most important element of the Tantric tradition; it is just one of many practices, which include yoga postures, breathing and meditation practices, and energy movement that channels Kundalini, the body's primal energy. Working with a partner serves to enhance these experiences, because the energy and consciousness of both people are combined.

In the Tantric worldview, sex was divinely created for committed couples to experience the transcendent while fully engaging in life—and without having to isolate themselves in an ascetic environment. Seen as a prayer practice, Tantric sex creates ecstatic present-moment consciousness, which induces feelings of oneness and deepened spiritual connection. In the experience of orgasm, practitioners do indeed die to everyday consciousness of themselves (which is why the French have labeled orgasm the *petit mort*, or "little death"), entering a state of bliss that can sometimes last for hours.

In fact, it is this widely rumored ability of Tantric-sex practitioners to extend their feelings of ecstasy that has spurred great interest among the uninitiated. Yet the rock star Sting was perhaps speaking for scores of people when he commented that when it was reported that he and his wife practiced Tantric sex for hours and hours, it wasn't mentioned that the time period included dinner and a movie.

Like all forms of prayer, intention behind the act is what distinguishes one practice from another as spiritual. As Dr. Deborah Anapol, founder of the Sacred Space Institute and a teacher of sacred sexuality, reminds us, "The dictionary defines sacred as 'made or *declared* holy, dedicated or devoted exclusively to a use, purpose, or person worthy of reverence or respect.'"

So whether one chooses the path of studying the ancient disciplines of Tantric sexuality, or holds sexual acts within a committed partnership with a new sense of its relationship to the sacred, what will transform the physical union is the precious ingredient of love. As Saint Francis de Sales wrote, "The soul cannot live without love."

Suggestions for Beginning the Exploration

- Again, knowing your intention for the practice is the most important place to start. What is it that draws you to this—deeper union with God, or with your partner? How you respond will affect how you proceed.
- Ways you can begin to create a spiritual container for your time with your partner include making the setting beautiful; dedicating your lovemaking as a holy experience; meditating and praying with your partner; gazing deeply into each other's eyes, moving slowly, and reserving an expanse of time; and infusing the experience with your love for your partner—and for God.

TEA CEREMONY

Genuine Peace Achieved through a Bowl of Tea

All of us who study chanoyu, through that practice, aim towards actualizing respect and harmony among people. At the same time, through the same practice, one's self and body are polished and reflected upon, and one's mind is brought to a state of clarity. Genuine peace, peace without discrimination, achieved through a bowl of tea—this is what I pray will be accomplished through the Way of Tea.

—HOUNSAI IEMOTO

Though both the Chinese and the Japanese have tea ceremonies, the Way of Tea is Japanese; it has been said that the difference between the two is that the Chinese emphasize the tea, while the Japanese emphasize the ceremony. And the ceremony is a prayer practice, having its roots in the tradition of Zen Buddhism.

The Japanese tea ceremony, called *chanoyu* or *chado*, involves—as its name implies—the act of preparing, serving, and drinking a powdered green tea called *macha*. But this is not about Martha Stewart-like detail, this is about spiritual metaphor and intent. According to Okakura Kakuzo, in his famous 1910 tract *The Book of Tea,*

> In chado, the spiritual aspect is most important. Harmony can be created between persons, between objects, between a person and an object.... In chado, we should respect everyone and everything without distinction of status or rank. In chado, spiritual purity is essential. We can embody tranquility only when we make harmony, respect, and purity our own. By learning chado, we seek to obtain an ultimate peace of mind. Chado is also deeply influenced by Zen thought. The ideal spirit of chado is a kind of religious mind. The essence of chado can be understood as the guiding principle for life for each person. The spirit of chado is universal.

Tea itself is said to have spiritual roots; Lao-tzu, the sixth-century founder of Taoism, was said to have been presented with the gift of tea by a disciple. And the legend in the Buddhist tradition is that when a great Buddhist saint was unable to meditate without getting drowsy, he cut off his eyelids and threw them to the ground. From them grew the eye-shaped leaves of the tea plant.

The green tea macha made its way to Japan in the twelfth century; and the tea ceremony as we know it today was first practiced by a Zen priest named Sen no Rikyu during the latter part of the sixteenth century. Rikyu's union of the most mundane acts of life with the most lofty spiritual ideals became what is known as the Way of Tea. In Rikyu's *Nambo Roku,* which addressed the tea ceremony's purpose and rules,

Rikyu compared the tea ceremony to the practice of the Buddha's teachings and the achievement of enlightenment. He explained that the ceremony's essence is "to simply carry the water, collect the wood, boil the water, and make the tea, offer it to the Buddha and share it with others."

Though Rikyu made it sound simple, there are intricate procedures for the tea ceremony, which is a symbolic representation of the fact that every encounter with others is one of a kind and will never occur in exactly the same way again. Because of the spiritual import of the ceremony, the tiniest detail is attended to in advance of—and during—the tea ceremony.

The tea ceremony is performed in a specially designated room for chado; the host's assistant and guests—ideally, there are four, one of whom is picked to be the "main guest"—must wash before entering the teahouse through a small sliding door. The low height of this door necessitates bowing or crouching, which emphasizes the equality of all participants. After entering, the guests, one by one, admire a scroll painting embellished with Buddhist scripture that has been chosen by the host to hang in the alcove.

If the tea ceremony involves a meal—called *chaji*—then every guest receives three courses. Like everything else in a tea ceremony, even the courses are symbolic; one is composed of seafood, to represent the bounty of the sea, and another is made of ingredients that represent the abundance of the land.

The water used to make tea represents yin; the fire that heats it, yang. The fresh water contained in a jar is touched only by the host, as it represents purity. A silk cloth symbolizes the spirit of the host, and is the tool used to purify the tea container.

The actions of the host illustrate a meditative art and are deeply important; they include the deliberate and mindful inspection, handling, examination, and cleaning of the tea utensils, each of which might be a valuable and expensive art piece. But the guests too have their rules to follow, such as gazing at the bowl, turning it, and wiping its rim.

All elements of Japanese art come into play during the tea ceremony, from architecture to flower arranging, ceramics to calligraphy. It has been suggested that not only has the tea ceremony affected these disciplines, but that it also was an essential influence on the polite manners of the Japanese people.

Is practicing the tea ceremony limited only to those who are Japanese? A Western tea enthusiast, Brother Joseph Keenan, thinks not: "Christians speak about experiencing Christ at the supper table; he can also be experienced at tea," he writes. "Jews speak of living out their covenant with God by keeping his law. Tea can be quite kosher. And Muslims can accept the will of Allah while sharing food and tea. Tea is for all nations, all cultures, and all religious traditions. . . .

"As the tea mind permeates more and more actions of your daily life, you may find yourself opening the china closet doors with more consciousness of that action at hand, and in a manner which strives for beauty in your movement. With that approach you may one day open those china closet doors only to realize that you have just opened the doors to the kingdom of heaven."

Suggestions for Beginning the Exploration

- Do you already conduct any ceremonies that involve others and that you could do more mindfully? For instance, if you have a regular gathering of people at your house, look for ways that you can consciously add elements to it that would deepen its meaning for you and the others.
- Explore how you can add more beauty to your everyday rituals and routines. Notice how being more mindful in your actions changes your experience of them—and see if your experience of your life also changes.

TECHNO-COSMIC MASS

Where Rave Meets Sacrament

Where rave meets sacrament,
and the posse is the priest.

—PROGRAM FOR A
TECHNO-COSMIC MASS

After entering the door from the street in downtown Oakland, California, you'll stand for a while in a narrow, dimly lit hallway that is painted blood red. When it is time for the worship service, you head up some stairs and enter a large, open space—formerly a ballroom—that holds up to 1,000 people. As you look around you, in every direction you see sensory stimuli: slides of various images in a colorful chain on all four walls; four different altars, one for each direction; a stage where vocalists and musicians perform; a sheer screen behind which dancers project their shadows. Welcome to the start of the Techno-Cosmic Mass.

Of all the prayer practices explored, the Techno-Cosmic Mass is one of the newest; it is an organic spiritual concoction whose ingredients initially consisted of youth, technology, dance, and dissatisfaction with traditional forms of worship. Interestingly, but perhaps not surprisingly, its roots lie in the ancient green land of Sheffield, England.

In the early 1980s, a number of young, progressive Anglicans felt a need to create a container that would be spacious enough for their love of their faith—and their love of techno-inspired music and dance. They started a group called the Nine O'Clock Service (NOS), held at St. Thomas Crookes Church in Sheffield. By the late 1980s, NOS had introduced Planetary Masses, conducted—as the group's name implies—every Sunday at 9 P.M. This new form of worship, the fledgling form of what was to become the Techno-Cosmic Mass, soon became much in demand.

The work of American author Matthew Fox, who became a priest in the Episcopal Church after being expelled from the Catholic Church for his nontraditional views, had reached the members of the Sheffield group, who by 1992 were captivated by Fox's theology. This interest in Fox's work was to influence the evolution of their unique worship ceremony.

In 1994, Fox brought the Planetary Mass—dubbed the Rave Mass by some, in reference to its similarities to the ecstatic rave dances that were becoming increasingly popular—to the United States. On Halloween weekend, the Planetary Mass debuted at San Francisco's Grace Cathedral; the invitation-only participants, who numbered three hundred, were said to include Jerry Garcia of the Grateful Dead. Among them were thirty-five people from Sheffield, who traveled to America to help produce the event. That night, at the

Planetary Mass, Fox reportedly said, "When a culture loses its spirituality, only the young can bring it back."

With time, the Planetary Mass has grown into the Techno-Cosmic Mass (TCM); according to TCM materials, *techno* refers to "the sacred use of technology in our worship"; *cosmic* refers to cosmology, "the sacred connection of all creation," and *mass* is identified as "an ancestral form of worship." It is a unique and enlivening blend of ritual dance, theater, and live music, incorporating recitation, elements of shamanism, and ubiquitous multimedia imagery.

Fox is also founder of the University of Creation Spirituality, which, according to its promotional materials, "seeks to integrate the wisdom of Western spirituality and global indigenous cultures with the emerging scientific understanding of the universe and passionate creativity of art [and] is concerned with renewing theologies and practices within religion and culture that promote personal wholeness, planetary survival, and universal interdependence." The concept of what Fox has developed in curriculum form and explored in books such as *Original Blessing*, the Four Paths are an integral part of the Techno-Cosmic Mass. Those four "paths," which divide the TCM into distinct sections, begin with the Via Positiva, in which participants gather, witness the invocation, and dance in praise. That is followed by the Via Negativa, a time of reflection, mourning by the community, and stillness. Then comes the Via Creativa, in which the participants share the peace and partake of the Eucharist; concluding with the Via Tranformativa, the final ecstatic dance before re-entering the world.

Because the philosophies behind the TCM can shift with each participant's experience and understanding, it can be helpful to observe how its promoters describe it themselves. For them, it is a celebration of the Cosmic Christ—"the pattern of Divine love and justice which exists in all of creation"—as well as the New Cosmology: The TCM is seen as "a microcosmic experience of the macrocosmic story." Additionally, the emphasis on movement "brings the body back to worship; trance dance is the primary form of prayer." With this, energy is moved, as "the TCM is designed to involve all seven chakras of the physical/spiritual body."

With a different theme celebrated during each TCM—focuses have included the Celtic Tradition, the Sacred Body, and Kinship with Animals—every worship experience is different. The constants are the organization around the Four Paths and the circular form of the Mass—participants flow around the center platform, consciously placed there to represent the "heart, womb, universal core from which all is birthed."

Because of its energy, its emphasis on communal participation, its attention to beauty, and its honoring of all faith paths—not to mention its chakra-stirring invitation to dance, laugh, wail, and pray—for many, the Techno-Cosmic Mass is a vehicle for transformation. This perhaps is fitting, as it exists itself as a symbol of transformation, a radical rewiring of a centuries-old tradition.

Suggestions for Beginning the Exploration

- If you were to create a spiritual ceremony that honored

your beliefs—and energized you to live by them—what music would you listen to? What dances would you move to? What readings would you include; what images would you want to look at? Would your ceremony be fast-paced, slow-paced, or a combination? Take note of the elements that come up for you in this reflection, and begin to incorporate them into your prayer life.

TREASURE MAPS

Illustrations of Your Soul's Autobiography

This is a meditative insight tool as well as a playmate, which means you want to bring your full concentration to each collage. Remember that these are the illustrations of your soul's autobiography. This is the first rough draft of your magnum opus . . . discovering who we are and why we are here at this point in eternity.

—SARAH BAN BREATHNACH

"The ancient Peruvians used to draw out their goals in symbols and paint them in primitive colors on the walls of caves," write Diane and Julia Loomans in their book *Full Esteem Ahead: 100 Ways to Teach Values and Build Self-Esteem for All Ages.* "The Egyptians used to create elaborate rituals to move from the state of desire to actualization. They believed that writing out a dream in advance would assure a positive outcome."

The customs of those early peoples were precursors of a contemporary prayer practice known by a number of names, including treasure maps, prosperity boards, and image books.

Some have suggested its relationship to the mandala, since treasure maps incorporate images to meditate upon. The difference—and it is a big one—is that treasure maps usually depict what one wants to have manifested in one's outer life, not what symbolizes the inner life. Like other prayer practices, treasure mapping can be secularized, and many people use it simply as a tool for establishing goals. Yet in a spiritual context, treasure maps become visual prayers, calling forth one's highest aspirations and ideals—a modern twist on the colorful symbols that the ancient Peruvians painted on cave walls.

As Lucia Cappachione writes in her illustrated book about treasure maps, *Visioning: Ten Steps to Designing the Life of Your Dreams,*

> We know from the work of C. G. Jung, Joseph Campbell, and countless others that the unconscious mind, feelings, intuitions, wishes, and dreams speak most truthfully in the language of images and symbols. . . . Designers know that to move from the realm of imagination into the material world, an idea must first be explored in tangible form: thumbnail sketch, diagram, mock-up, or blueprint. . . . Looking at [treasure maps] repeatedly after they are completed burns the image into the brain and the memory.

Given that important "why"—because they have an energetic life of their own, and can assist individuals in seeing greater possibilities for their lives—there are a number of ways to go about the "how." A treasure map is simply a collage, a collection of pictures that you select for inspiration and glue onto a background. The components are simple: posterboard or paper, scissors, glue, words and images cut out of magazines. You can also use markers, pastels, paints, or crayons to write affirmations or prayers on your treasure map.

What you place on your treasure map should have deep significance for you; incorporate colors and pictures that particularly please you. If you want, you can photocopy photographs of yourself—or use actual snapshots—to accentuate the sense of this vision being yours. Try not to censor yourself; this is not the time to tell yourself to be "more realistic." You are creating your vision for the future, so dream big.

You can do generally themed treasure maps—one depicting a number of elements in your life, including your ideal career, relationship goals, and desired health and fitness levels—or you can make them specific. Possibilities in this category could include treasure-mapping a project that you're working on, such as writing a book; a goal you want to meet, such as running a marathon; or a personal challenge that you want to overcome, such as losing forty pounds.

Others recommend doing treasure maps in book form. Author Sarah Ban Breathnach has created a bound book called *The Illustrated Discovery Journal,* with sections that include "Authentic Style," "Return to Self," "Sacred Connections," and "Someday." If you'd rather create your own binder, the publishers of the *Master Mind Journal* recommend creating an "Image Book," in which you do an individual treasure map for at least eight areas of your life: physical, mental, relationships, travel, career, prosperity, self-esteem, and spiritual growth.

Cappachione, however, feels that it's better to stick with a single area of focus, and then progress to the next. In an interview for borders.com, she said, "I suggest that they just stick with one wish at a time and as that wish starts to manifest, then they can start doing a collage for another one. If you've got too many pots on the stove, I think it just gets too confusing for the psyche."

Whatever you choose to do, it's helpful to construct some sort of container for working with your treasure maps. For some people, it's an annual or semi-annual ritual, and they look forward to doing it on New Year's Day or on their birthday. For others, it's an ongoing practice, and treasure maps are created as the individuals feel called to make them.

People who do this as a spiritual practice recommend spending regular time with one's treasure map—to meditate upon its words and images for at least ten minutes in the morning and in the evening. It should be placed in a very visible location, so that its images are accessible to you throughout the day. If you have a personal altar, that is an ideal location for your treasure map; you can enfold it into your prayer and meditation time.

You can also do treasure maps that focus on spiritual aspirations—a characteristic that you would like to embody, such as compassion or patience—and select images that will support you: pictures of Kuan Yin, Jesus, angels. Say prayers as you look at it, then affirm that your prayers will be answered by concluding with one of thanksgiving. There is something about seeing the visual representation of what we hope to become—and really entering that vision, really feeling how it would be to obtain that vision—that affects our lives in a powerful and tangible way.

Suggestions for Beginning the Exploration

- Begin to think about your prayers for your life. Do you want to meet your soulmate? Find work that contributes to others? Have a child? Begin to collect words and images that speak to this desire, and create a treasure map.
- Place your treasure map on your altar, keep it in your prayer journal, or hold it during your prayer time. Note how your treasure map changes your prayer life.

Vision Quests

Finding Tongues in Trees, Sermons in Stones

And this our life,
exempt from public haunts
finds tongues in trees,
books in the running brooks,
sermons in stones
and good in every thing.

—William Shakespeare

Though spiritual leaders from almost every major religious tradition have modeled the experience of a vision quest—including Jesus and Moses, who each spent forty days in isolation to fast and pray, as well as Buddha and Mohammed—the term "vision quest" is associated with Native Americans and was coined by nineteenth-century anthropologists studying their ceremonies. The concept of a vision quest has not only spiritual roots, but also psychological; it is the enactment of the hero's journey, an archetypal ritual that calls its practitioners to face literal and metaphorical darkness, alone, in order to discover the light within. A vision quest enables us to "die" to old ways and be reborn into the new.

Today, there is a new wave of interest in vision quests from those outside the Native American culture, but it is crucial that we hold their particular rituals with great respect. We use the same phrase for a prayer practice that may have similar components, but we need to acknowledge the important ceremonial differences. For Native Americans, the vision quest, or *hanblecheyapi*—which translates "crying for a vision"—is a means to seek divine guidance or acquire a guardian spirit. Doing this in nature is an integral part of the practice; writes Ed McGaa, Eagle Man, "Why not spend at least a day and night of serious, uninterrupted prayer and communication with the powers of the universe in the greatest temple of all—out in God's created nature under God's vast heavens. No church or building can give such visualization of the Great Mystery's magnitude." It is first practiced when an adolescent boy enters puberty; although, in some tribes, girls also undergo a period of isolation at the time they start menstruating. During the quest, the guardian spirit—often in animal form—is made known during a vision, visitation, or dream. Identifying with and cultivating the powers of that animal provides the individual with a sense of personal purpose and strength.

Later, vision quests are done during times of transition with the intention of improving oneself or one's health, or to serve one's community by bringing back a vision for a particular challenge. Because of the sacredness of this ritual, practitioners purify themselves in a sweat lodge before a vision quest; once the person is on the quest, he or she usually fasts and prays.

All these elements of the vision quest heighten the individual's experience, as they eliminate any additional distractions and physiologically sharpen one's perception. As is common in a spiritual and psychological journey, the quest is done in stages: the first is severance, as one leaves the old way of being; the second is the threshold, where one experiences transformation; and the third is incorporation, in which one brings the vision back into the world in order to make it better.

As the following story shows, the vision quest experience is not limited to the time a person spends alone in nature; it begins to influence that person in the time preceding it, and its reverberations affect the quester long after he or she has emerged from that sacred time and place. For Molly Starr, a writer and marketing director for an international e-consulting firm, going on a vision quest—a mandatory experience in a yearlong class Molly was taking—changed her life. "I had just turned sixty when I had my first vision quest," she laughs. "I was a virgin! I experienced a great deal of excitement about it, because my most creative times are when I'm isolated. I was also frightened, because I was going to be alone for a long period of time.

"The week before we went on the vision quest, I opened up the paper, and there was an article about the heat wave we were experiencing—that it had driven rattlesnakes out into the open, and a man had been badly bitten. All of a sudden I was afraid of snakes, and yet I knew that they were a foil for what was really going on inside of me—this fear about a new experience. I had done a lot of camping, but never alone. As the days led up to it, it felt like Gethsemane—I wanted to do it, and I was afraid, and I had no idea what the outcome would be. It definitely felt like a spiritual journey.

"The first full day of the quest, I found this place on the mountain, pitched my tent, and put my rope around it—my teacher had instructed us to bring fifty feet of coarse rope to surround our tent with, as snakes don't like that rough feeling on their bellies. Just to make sure, I brought a hundred feet of rope, so I had two rings around me. Then I went into my tent and fell asleep. And I slept the rest of the day and through the night. And I felt held by the earth, perfectly safe.

"When I woke up the morning of the second day, I heard movement outside the tent—and it was a wild-turkey mother with a dozen baby chicks following her. And the lizards were leaping, and the birds were eating, and everything was going about its business. And I was ecstatic. And the ecstasy was for the life that I saw—everything was so beautiful: the freaky, frenetic little lizards, the wild turkey mother—and I realized I was in the moment, I was entirely in the moment. And I spent the rest of the day in the moment—it was a day of prayer and meditation in the woods.

"That night I went to sleep, and again I felt cradled, like I was held in the hand of God—like a little animal, safe in its burrow. At 1:25 in the morning—I looked at my watch—I woke up. I had had a healing dream of great proportion, which was a surprise to me, because I had not expected it. And in the dream I was able to see my own disease, my own instability, and the damage to my soul. And I was able in the dream to acknowledge that and forgive it. It was absolutely astounding—I knew it was important. And the next morning I had come to full acceptance of who I was, and with that acceptance there was no blame: everyone was forgiven, including myself. I let go, and just gave it to God. I think it was the pinnacle of my own spiritual life.

"You're in a state of prayer the entire time during a vision quest; the entire experience is a prayer practice. Sounds were sharpened, colors were brighter, the air was clearer—and I had an extraordinary sense of well-being and connection to everything. Today, it still helps me—I go back there; I remember that experience in my daily prayer time.

"And there was an epiphany with the snakes! The final morning, when I woke up, I found myself thinking very positively about snakes, and longing to see one. I was filled with the sense that snakes were my ally; that it was through my ability to compartmentalize my fear onto snakes that I had the experience I did. They had held my fear for me; and since I hadn't seen one during my vision quest, I could have those divine moments. I realized that the snake was my greatest friend, because that is something very powerful to do for someone else.

"I was in an altered state of consciousness when I came down that mountain—I was euphoric. Within a few weeks, I started writing again—after an eight-year hiatus—and I started doing artwork again. For me, the spiritual connection allowed that creativity."

Molly's experience of reconnecting to her creativity mirrors what many people discover after their vision quest. As Ed McGaa explains, "The quest is very personal. It is you and your thoughts and your prayers to the Great Spirit. . . . Afterward, you, the vision quester, will be better prepared to use the special gifts with which the Great Spirit has endowed you to join with those concerned ones who seek to help this planet."

Suggestions for Beginning the Exploration

- First, be clear: Where will you go? When? For how long? Why are you going? Second, be open: Don't anticipate or expect anything—allow your experience to unfold the way it's meant to.
- Make sure you are accompanied in the outdoors by someone who is experienced. The process of vision questing is an intense one, and you owe it to yourself to have a safe container provided by knowledgeable guides both during your quest and after it.
- Treat the area you're in with tender care. Leave it as you found it; remove any trash that might have been there before your arrival; and honor it with a gift when you leave—a pinch of tobacco or corn.
- Bring only what you need; leave all possible distractions at home. Take advantage of this precious time to be alone with yourself and your God.
- Make the time meaningful; watch attentively for animal, reptile, and insect visitors, and pay attention to their behaviors. Allow your mind to make symbolic

associations. You can fast—making sure to drink plenty of water—or not; you can sleep during the day, or not at all. This is your time; do what you feel called to do.

VISUAL ARTS

The Work of Body and Soul

All great art is the work of the whole living creature, body and soul, and chiefly of the soul.

—JOHN RUSKIN

Albert Einstein once wrote that "the most beautiful thing we can experience is the mysterious. It is the source of all true art and science"—and, he might well have added, it is the source of true faith. Given this connection between faith and art, the practice of bringing forth something in tangible form that has never existed before is a prayer, a communion with God, of the highest magnitude. By creating, we glimpse the spark of the Creator in ourselves; or, as feminist theologian Mary Daly wrote, "It is the creative potential itself in human beings that is the image of God."

Art has been used throughout time by people to honor the sacred: from the woven ojos, or "God's eyes," made by ancient Egyptians and still made today as a symbol that God is watching over us, to elaborate gem-encrusted icons and the Buddhist *tankhas* painted on silk depicting deities both inviting and frightening. Each of these images inspires its viewers;

each asks us to consider lifting a veil, to see the spiritual beckoning underneath.

In Islam, all things of beauty reflect the Divine, and thus all art is spiritual. But because the Creator is seen as the only one who can create, Islamic decoration is limited to pattern—it is forbidden by the Koran to depict animals or humans. Yet even the great Sufi poet Rumi urged that:

> Inside you there's an artist you
> don't know about . . . Say yes
> quickly, if you know, if
> you've known it from before the
> beginning of the universe.

In Rollo May's book *The Courage to Create,* the writer explores the artist's ability to lose track of time and even place, to become so lost in the present moment that he or she has in fact entered a new dimension of experience. Furthermore, in the act of creating, the artist taps into something deeper, like a living stream under the ice: "What genuine painters do is to reveal the underlying psychological and spiritual conditions of their relationship to their world; thus in the works of a great painter we have a reflection of the emotional and spiritual condition of human beings in that period of history." Even more nourishing is when the conscious intention of the artist is to invoke a sense of the sacred for others—as contemporary painter and writer Alex Grey has explored in his books as the highest intent for an artist. He has even composed an "Artist's Prayer," whose last stanza asks that the work be infused by spirit, in order "to feed hungry souls."

It is this feeding of hungry souls that makes art transformative, though it has always been a matter of interpretation what exactly might do that. One artist who attempted to do so was Wassily Kandinsky, who, in his *Concerning the Spiritual in Art,* wrote, "Painting is an art . . . a power which must be directed to the improvement and refinement of the human soul. . . . If art refrains from doing this work, a chasm remains unbridged, for no other power can take the place of art in this activity. And at times when the human soul is gaining greater strength, art will also grow in power, for the two are inextricably connected and complementary one to the other."

The process of creating—and we are all artists of one form or another—is one in which we enter an altered state, a pocket of timeless, placeless existence where the only focus is on the object being created. The artist infuses his or her energy into the creation; the creation comes alive in ways the artist could not have anticipated; this blended energy of creator and created affects the energy within the viewer in a circle of experience. As the spiritual adage goes, when the potter makes the pot, what's being shaped is the potter.

As art therapist and author Lucia Cappachione writes in *The Soul of Creativity,*

> Like the source of all creation, you are a creator, too. It is your divine birthright. The person who says "I'm not creative" is uttering blasphemy. The truth is that you are the Creative Self expressing through the human vessel of your body, emotions, mind, and soul. . . .

In embracing creativity as our spiritual practice, we commend ourselves into the Creator's hands, knowing that our goal is to disappear. And when we do, we become one with all creation.

Suggestions for Beginning the Practice

- Even if you don't think of yourself as an artist, begin to bring art materials into your prayer time. Instead of praying in words, pray in pictures. What colors are you drawn to, what shapes and intensities? Try keeping a journal or notebook containing these visual prayers.
- Pay attention to the visual representations of the Sacred that move you. Why do they—what is it you respond to? Exploring these reasons will paint a symbolic picture of how you view the Divine.

ACKNOWLEDGMENTS

My thanks to all at Conari Press, particularly Leslie Berriman, a truly thoughtful and sensitive editor, and Brenda Knight, for her energy and enthusiasm. Many thanks also to Alan Jones, for the wonderful contribution of his foreword.

I am blessed with an incredible circle of family members, friends, and colleagues, and I am so grateful to all of them for their inspiration and support. Special thanks go to my husband, Scott, to whom this book is dedicated and without whom it might not have been written; my mother, Jane Oman; Laurie Bish Evans; Susan Ariel Rainbow Kennedy; Faith Meenan; and the radiant Molly Starr.

It was an honor and privilege to interview the following people, who gave us all the gift of sharing the intimacies of their prayer life: Lynn Baskfield, Ilene Cummings, Joan Currey, John deValcourt, Holly Downes, Louise Dunn, Ann Keeler Evans, Peg Grady, Gail C. Jones, Athena Katsaros, Kathy Kidd, Caterina Rando, Celeste Smeland, Molly Starr, Eleanor Wiley, and Bruce Zuckerman. My deepest thanks to all of them.

Above all, I am grateful to God for the many gifts of my life, including the opportunity to celebrate Spirit through this book. It is my prayer that all those who contributed to it, directly and indirectly, and all those who read it will be deeply blessed.

FOR FURTHER READING

AFFIRMATIONS

Bloch, Douglas. *Words That Heal: Affirmations and Meditations for Daily Living*. New York: Bantam Books, 1990.

Harman, Willis, and Howard Rheingold. *Higher Creativity: Liberating the Unconscious for Breakthrough Insights*. New York: Jeremy P. Tarcher/Perigee Books, 1984.

Hay, Louise. *Heal Your Body*. Carlsbad, CA: Hay House, 1997.

Yogananda, Paramahansa. *Scientific Healing Affirmations*. Los Angeles: Self-Realization Fellowship, 2000.

ALTARS

Linn, Denise. *Altars: Bringing Sacred Shrines into Your Everyday Life*. New York: Ballantine Wellspring, 1999.

McMann, Jean. *Altars and Icons: Sacred Spaces in Everyday Life*. San Francisco: Chronicle Books, 1998.

Searl, Edward. *A Place of Your Own*. New York: Berkley Books, 1998.

Streep, Peg. *Altars Made Easy: A Complete Guide to Creating Your Own Sacred Space*. New York: HarperSanFrancisco, 1997.

AMULETS

Kunz, George Frederick. *The Magic of Jewels and Charms.* Mineola, NY: Dover Publications, 1997.

ANGELS

Burnham, Sophy. *A Book of Angels.* New York: Ballantine Books, 1990.

Godwin, Malcolm. *Angels: An Endangered Species.* New York: Simon & Schuster, 1990

BODY PRAYER

Moroni, Giancarlo. *My Hands Held Out to You: The Use of Body and Hands in Prayer.* New York: Paulist Press, 1992.

Vennard, Jane E. *Praying with Body and Soul.* Minneapolis: Augsburg Fortress Publishers, 1998.

Wuellner, Flora Slosson. *Prayer and Our Bodies.* Nashville, TN: Upper Room, 1987.

CENTERING PRAYER

Johnston, William, ed. *The Cloud of Unknowing.* New York: Image Books/Doubleday, 1973.

CHANTS

Gass, Robert, with Kathleen Brehony. *Chanting: Discovering Spirit in Sound.* New York: Broadway Books, 1999.

Prayer: A Multi-Cultural Journey of Spirit (CD by Soundings of the Planet, 1-800-93-PEACE)

EXAMEN OF CONSCIENCE

Champlin, Joseph M. "Look into Your Heart: An Examination of Conscience." Liguori, MO: Liguori Publications, 1998.

Twelve Steps and Twelve Traditions. New York: Alcoholics Anonymous World Services, Inc., 1996.

FEASTS

Kesten, Deborah. *Feeding the Body, Nourishing the Soul*. Berkeley, CA: Conari Press, 1997.

FOOD MEDITATIONS

Altman, Donald. *Art of the Inner Meal: Eating as a Spiritual Path*. New York: HarperSanFrancisco, 1999.

David, Marc. *Nourishing Wisdom: A Mind-Body Approach to Nutrition and Well-Being*. New York: Bell Tower, 1991.

Harper, Linda R. *The Tao of Eating: Feeding Your Soul through Everyday Experiences with Food*. Philadephia, PA: Innisfree Press, 1998.

Kabat-Zinn, Jon. *Full Catastrophe Living*. New York: Dell Publishing, 1990.

Kabatznick, Ronna. *The Zen of Eating: Ancient Answers to Modern Weight Problems*. New York: Perigree, 1998.

Nhat Hanh, Thich. *Touching Peace: Practicing the Art of Mindful Living*. Berkeley, CA: Parallax Press, 1992.

FORMAL PRAYERS

Oman, Maggie, ed. *Prayers for Healing*. Berkeley, CA: Conari Press, 1997.

Ryan, M. J., ed. *A Grateful Heart*. Berkeley, CA: Conari Press, 1994.

GRATITUDE AND PRAYER JOURNALS

Ban Breathnach, Sarah. *Simple Abundance: A Daybook of Comfort and Joy*. New York: Warner Books, 1995.

Beattie, Melody. *Gratitude: Affirming the Good Things in Life.* Center City, MN: Hazelden, 1992.

Klug, Ronald. *How to Keep a Spiritual Journal.* Nashville, TN: Thomas Nelson Publishers, 1982.

Steindl-Rast, David. *Gratefulness, The Heart of Prayer.* New York: Paulist Press, 1984.

GUIDES

Andrews, Ted. *Animal-Speak.* St. Paul, MN: Llewellyn Publications, 1995.

Andrews, Ted. *How to Meet and Work with Spirit Guides.* St. Paul, MN: Llewellyn Publications, 1997.

Bennett, Hal Zina. *Zuni Fetishes.* New York: HarperSanFrancisco, 1993.

McElroy, Susan Chernak. *Animals as Teachers and Healers.* Troutdale, OR: NewSage Press, 1996.

Saunders, Nicholas J. *Animal Spirits.* Boston: Little, Brown and Company, 1995.

Steiger, Brad. *Totems: The Transformative Power of Your Personal Animal Totem.* New York: HarperSanFrancisco, 1997.

HAIKU

Van den Heuvel, Cor. *The Haiku Anthology.* New York: Fireside/Simon & Schuster, 1986.

IKEBANA

Davey, H. E., and Ann Kameoka. *The Japanese Way of the Flower: Ikebana as Moving Meditation.* Berkeley, CA: Stone Bridge Press, 2000.

INSTRUMENTAL MUSIC

Redmond, Layne. *When the Drummers Were Women: A Spiritual History of Rhythm.* New York: Three Rivers Press, 1997.

LABYRINTHS AND PRAYER-WALKING

Kortge, Carolyn Scott. *The Spirited Walker.* New York: HarperSanFrancisco, 1998.

Mundy, Linus. *The Complete Guide to Prayer-Walking.* New York: The Crossroad Publishing Company, 1996.

MANDALAS

Cornell, Judith. *Mandala: Luminous Symbols for Healing.* Wheaton, IL: Quest Books, 1994.

Fincher, Susanne F. *Creating Mandalas: For Insight, Healing and Self-Expression.* Boston: Shambhala, 1991.

MASTER MIND GROUPS

Master Mind Journal. Published each calendar year by the Master Mind Publishing Company, 1-800-256-1984.

MEDITATION AND BREATHING PRACTICES

Easwaran, Eknath. *Meditation.* Tomales, CA: Nilgiri Press, 1991.

Goldsmith, Joel S. *The Art of Meditation.* New York: Harper & Row, 1990.

Osho. *The Everyday Meditator.* Boston: Charles E. Tuttle Co. Inc., 1993.

Ozaniec, Naomi. *Basic Meditation.* New York: Dorling Kindersley, 1997.

MILAGROS

Thompson, Helen. *Milagros: A Book of Miracles*. New York: HarperSanFrancisco, 1998.

PERSONAL SACRED TEXT

Barks, Coleman, and Michael Green. *The Illuminated Rumi*. New York: Broadway Books, 1997.

Parish, Bobbi L. *Create Your Personal Sacred Text*. New York: Broadway Books, 1999.

Sandra Kahn's workshop can be accessed at *www.spiritualityhealth.com/life/course1.html.*

PRAYER BEADS

Pennington, M. Basil. *Praying by Hand*. New York: HarperSanFrancisco, 1991.

Tomalin, Stefany. *The Bead Jewelry Book*. Chicago: Contemporary Books, 1998.

PRAYER BOWLS

Rupp, Joyce. *The Cup of Our Life: A Guide for Spiritual Growth*. Notre Dame, IN: Ave Maria Press, 1997.

PRAYER DANCING

Roth, Gabrielle. *Sweat Your Prayers: Movement as Spiritual Practice*. New York: Jeremy P. Tarcher/Putnam, 1997.

PRAYER FLAGS

For more about making a calendar conversion, see *http://www.snowlionpub.com/pages/prayerflags.html.*

For more information on the prayer flags for women with breast cancer, see *www.breastcancerprayerflags.org*.

PRAYER RUGS

Barks, Coleman, and Michael Green. *The Illuminated Prayer.* New York: Ballantine Wellspring, 2000.

PRAYER WITH OTHERS

Virtue, Doreen, Ph.D. *The Lightworker's Way: Awakening Your Spiritual Power to Know and Heal.* Carlsbad, CA: Hay House, 1997.

RITUALS

Beck, Renee, and Sydney Barbara Metrick. *The Art of Ritual: A Guide to Creating and Performing Your Own Rituals for Growth and Change.* Berkeley, CA: Celestial Arts, 1990.

Biziou, Barbara. *The Joy of Ritual.* New York: Golden Books, 1999.

Paladin, Lynda S. *Ceremonies for Change: Creating Personal Ritual to Heal Life's Hurts.* Walpole, NH: Stillpoint Publishing, 1991.

Pollack, Rachel. *The Power of Ritual.* New York: Dell Publishing, 2000.

Walker, Barbara G. *Women's Rituals: A Sourcebook.* New York: HarperSanFrancisco, 1990.

SACRED SCRIPTURES

Andersen, Frank. *Imagine Jesus. . . .* Ligouri, MO: Ligouri Publications, 1996.

Novak, Philip. *The World's Wisdom: Sacred Texts of the World's Religions.* Edison, NJ: Castle Books, 1996.

SAINTS

Buono, Anthony M. "Praying with the Saints." Liguori, MO: Liguori Publications, 1999.

Cowan, Tom. *The Way of the Saints: Prayers, Practices and Meditations*. New York: G. P. Putnam's Sons, 1998.

Ellsberg, Robert. *All Saints*. New York: The Crossroad Publishing Company, 1999.

Hallam, Elizabeth. *Saints: Who They Are and How They Help You*. New York: Simon & Schuster, 1994.

Hutchinson, Gloria. *Six Ways to Pray from Six Great Saints*. Cincinnati, OH: St. Anthony Messenger Press, 1982.

Schlesinger, Henry. *Everyday Saints: A Guide to Special Prayers*. New York: Avon, 1996.

SHADOW WORK

Ford, Debbie. *The Dark Side of the Light Chasers: Reclaiming Your Power, Creativity, Brilliance, and Dreams*. New York: Riverhead Books, 1998.

Zweig, Connie, and Steve Wolf. *Romancing the Shadow: Illuminating the Dark Side of the Soul*. New York: Ballantine Books, 1997.

STORYTELLING

Estés, Clarissa Pinkola. *The Gift of Story*. New York: Ballantine Books, 1993.

Gilmour, Peter. *The Wisdom of Memoir: Reading and Writing Life's Sacred Texts*. Winona, MN: Saint Mary's Press, 1997.

Kurtz, Ernest, and Katherine Ketcham. *The Spirituality of Imperfection: Storytelling and the Journey to Wholeness*. New York: Bantam Books, 1994.

Maguire, Jack. *The Power of Personal Storytelling: Spinning Tales to Connect with Others*. New York: Jeremy P. Tarcher/Putnam, 1998.

McKenna, Megan, and Tony Cowan. *Keepers of the Story*. Maryknoll, NY: Orbis Books, 1997.

SWEAT LODGES

McGaa, Ed, "Eagle Man." *Mother Earth Spirituality: Native American Paths to Healing Ourselves and Our World.* New York: HarperSanFrancisco, 1990.

TANTRIC SEX

LaCroix, Nitya. *The Art of Tantric Sex.* New York: Dorling Kindersley, 1997.

TEA CEREMONY

Lee, Anthony Man-Tu. *The Japanese Tea Ceremony.* Boston: Element Books, 1999.

TECHNO-COSMIC MASS

Fox, Matthew. *Original Blessing.* Santa Fe, NM: Bear & Company, 1983.

TREASURE MAPS

Ban Breathnach, Sarah. *The Illustrated Discovery Journal: Creating a Visual Autobiography of Your Authentic Self.* New York: WarnerBooks, 1999.

Cappacchione, Lucia. *Visioning: Ten Steps to Designing the Life of Your Dreams.* New York: Jeremy P. Tarcher/Putnam, 2000.

VISION QUESTS

Cruden, Loren. *Spirit of Place: A Workbook for Sacred Alignment.* Rochester, VT: Destiny Books, 1995.

McLuhan, T. C. *Cathedrals of the Spirit: The Message of Sacred Places.* Toronto: HarperCollins, 1996.

VISUAL ARTS

Boulet, Susan Seddon. *Shaman*. San Francisco: Pomegranate Artbooks, 1989.

Crockett, Tom. *The Artist Inside: A Spiritual Guide to Cultivating Your Creative Self*. New York: Broadway Books, 2000.

Fischer, Kathleen R. *The Inner Rainbow: The Imagination in Christian Life*. New York: Paulist Press, 1983.

Kandinsky, Wassily. *Concerning the Spiritual in Art*. New York: Dover Publications, 1977.

Myers, Tona Pearce, ed. *The Soul of Creativity: Insights into the Creative Process*. Novato, CA: New World Library, 1999.

SARK. *A Creative Companion*. Berkeley, CA: Celestial Arts, 1991.

SELECT BIBLIOGRAPHY

Aitken, Robert, and David Steindl-Rast. *The Ground We Share: Everyday Practice, Buddhist and Christian.* Ligouri, MO: Triumph Books, 1994.

Angell, Carole S. *Celebrations around the World: A Multicultural Handbook.* Golden, CO: Fulcrum Publishing, 1996.

Arrien, Angeles. *The Four-Fold Way.* New York: HarperSanFrancisco, 1993.

Bottorff, J. Douglas. *A Practical Guide to Meditation and Prayer.* Unity Village, MO: Unity Books, 1990.

Bowes, Susan. *Life Magic.* New York: Simon & Schuster Editions, 1999.

Bruce-Mitford, Miranda. *The Illustrated Book of Signs and Symbols.* New York: Dorling Kindersley, 1996.

Brussat, Frederic and Mary Ann. *Spiritual Literacy: Reading the Sacred in Everyday Life.* New York: Scribner, 1996.

Crim, Keith, ed. *The Perennial Dictionary of World Religions.* New York: HarperSanFrancisco, 1989.

Davies, Susan Shannon. *15 Ways to Nourish Your Faith.* New York: Paulist Press, 1998.

Davis, Avram, ed. *Meditation from the Heart of Judaism.* Woodstock, VT: Jewish Lights Publishing, 1997.

Dossey, Larry, and other contributors, with Michael Toms. *The Power of Meditation and Prayer.* Carlsbad, CA: Hay House, 1997.

Editors at Skylight Paths. *The New Millennium Spiritual Journey.* Woodstock, VT: Skylight Paths Publishing, 1999.

Edwards, Tilden. *Living in the Presence: Spiritual Exercises to Open Our Lives to the Awareness of God.* New York: HarperSanFrancisco, 1994.

Egeberg, Gary. *The Pocket Guide to Prayer.* Minneapolis, MN: Augsburg Fortress, 1999.

Eliade, Mircea. *From Primitives to Zen: A Thematic Sourcebook of the History of Religions.* San Francisco: Harper & Row, 1977.

Ensley, Eddie. *Prayer That Heals Our Emotions.* San Francisco: Harper & Row, 1988.

Feuerstein, George, and Stephan Bodian. *Living Yoga: A Comprehensive Guide for Daily Life.* New York: Jeremy P. Tarcher/Perigree, 1993.

Fontana, David. *The Secret Language of Symbols.* San Francisco: Chronicle Books, 1993.

Freke, Timothy. *Encyclopedia of Spirituality.* New York: Godsfield Press, 2000.

___. *The Wisdom of the Hindu Gurus.* Boston: Godsfield Press, 1998.

___. *The Wisdom of the Sufi Sages.* Boston: Godsfield Press, 1998.

___. *The Wisdom of the Tibetan Lamas.* Boston: Godsfield Press, 1998.

___. *The Wisdom of the Zen Masters.* Boston: Godsfield Press, 1998.

Freke, Timothy, and Peter Gandy. *The Complete Guide to World Mysticism.* London: Piatkus, 1997.

George, Mike. *Discover Inner Peace: A Guide to Spiritual Well-Being.* San Francisco: Chronicle Books, 2000.

Goring, Rosemary, ed. *Larousse Dictionary of Beliefs and Religions.* New York: Larousse, 1994.

Harner, Michael. *The Way of the Shaman.* New York: HarperSanFrancisco, 1990.

Holy Bible: New International Version. Grand Rapids, MI: Zondervan Publishing House, 1984.

Hope, Jane. *The Secret Language of Soul: A Visual Guide to the Spiritual World.* San Francisco: Chronicle Books, 1997.

Huxley, Francis. *The Way of the Sacred.* London: Bloomsbury Books, 1989.

Ingpen, Robert, and Philip Wilkinson. *A Celebration of Customs and Rituals of the World.* New York: Facts on File, Inc., 1996.

Interreligious Council of San Diego. *Bridging Our Faiths.* New York: Paulist Press, 1997.

Jordan, Michael. *Encyclopedia of Gods: Over 2,500 Deities of the World.* New York: Facts on File, Inc., 1993.

Jung, Carl G. *Man and His Symbols.* New York: Doubleday & Co., 1964.

____. *Psychology and Religion.* Binghamton, NY: The Vail-Ballou Press, Inc., 1978.

Kelsey, Morton. *Spiritual Living in a Material World: A Practical Guide.* Hyde Park, NY: New City Press, 1998.

King, Francis X. *Mind and Magic.* New York: Crescent Books, 1991.

Kornfield, Jack. *A Path with Heart: A Guide through the Perils and Promises of Spiritual Life.* New York: Bantam Books, 1993.

Lash, John. *The Seeker's Handbook: The Complete Guide to Spiritual Pathfinding.* New York: Harmony Books, 1990.

Leder, Drew. *Games for the Soul.* New York: Hyperion, 1998.

L'Engle, Madeleine. *Walking on Water: Reflections on Faith and Art.* Wheaton, IL: Harold Shaw Publishers, 1980.

Moses, Jeffrey. *Oneness: Great Principles Shared by All Religions.* New York: Fawcett Columbine, 1989.

Nouwen, Henri J. M. *With Open Hands*. New York: Ballantine Books, 1985.

Novak, Philip. *The World's Wisdom: Sacred Texts of the World's Religions*. Edison, NJ: Castle Books, 1996.

Oliver, Joan Duncan. *Contemplative Living*. New York: Dell Publishing, 2000.

Parrinder, Geoffrey, ed. *World Religions: From Ancient History to the Present*. New York: Facts on File, Inc., 1971.

Philip, Neil. *The Illustrated Book of Myths*. New York: Dorling Kindersley, 1995.

Putík, Alexandr, and other contributors. *Jewish Customs and Traditions*. Prague: State Jewish Museum in Prague, 1992.

Sakya, Jnan Bahadur. *Short Description of Gods, Goddesses and Ritual Objects of Buddhism and Hinduism in Nepal*. Nepal: Handicraft Association of Nepal, 1999.

Salwak, Dale, ed. *The Power of Prayer.* Novato, CA: New World Library, 1998.

Sherley-Price, Leo, trans. *Thomas á Kempis: Counsels on the Spiritual Life*. New York: Penguin Books, 1995.

Shideler, Mary McDermott. *In Search of the Spirit: A Primer.* New York: Ballantine/Epiphany, 1985.

Shield, Benjamin, and Richard Carlson. *For the Love of God: Handbook for the Spirit*. Novato, CA: New World Library, 1997.

Smith, Huston. *The Illustrated World's Religions: A Guide to Our Wisdom Traditions*. New York: HarperSanFrancisco, 1994.

Smith, Jonathan Z., and William Scott Green. *The HarperCollins Dictionary of Religion*. New York: HarperSanFrancisco, 1995.

Steindl-Rast, David. *A Listening Heart: The Art of Contemplative Living*. New York: Crossroad, 1994.

Steltenkamp, Michael F. *The Sacred Vision: Native American Religion and Its Practice Today.* New York: Paulist Press, 1982.

St. Romain, Philip. *Pathways to Serenity.* Ligouri, MO: Ligouri Publications, 1998.

Tomlinson, Gerald. *Treasury of Religious Quotations.* Englewood Cliffs, NJ: Prentice Hall, 1991.

Twelve Steps and Twelve Traditions. New York: Alcoholics Anonymous World Services, Inc., 1996.

Virtue, Doreen. *The Lightworker's Way: Awakening Your Spiritual Power to Know and Heal.* Carlsbad, CA: Hay House, 1997.

Walsh, Mary Caswell. *The Art of Tradition: A Christian Guide to Building a Family.* Denver, CO: The Morehouse Publishing Group, 1998.

Walsh, Roger. *Essential Spirituality: The 7 Central Practices to Awaken Heart and Mind.* New York: John Wiley & Sons, 1999.

Zaleski, Philip, and Paul Kaufman. *Gifts of the Spirit: Living the Wisdom of the Great Religious Traditions.* New York: HarperSanFrancisco, 1997.

Zerah, Aaron. *The Soul's Almanac: A Year of Interfaith Stories, Prayers and Wisdom.* New York: Jeremy P. Tarcher/Putnam, 1998.

Zubko, Andy. *Treasury of Spiritual Wisdom.* San Diego: Blue Dove Press, 1998.

INDEX

C

D

E

F

G

H

I

J

K

L

T

U

V

W

Y

Z

ABOUT THE AUTHOR

Maggie Oman Shannon is a spiritual director and writer with a special interest in practices that nourish the soul. She is the editor of *Prayers for Healing*, an anthology of prayers from around the world, published by Conari Press in 1997. The former editor of three national magazines, including *The Saturday Evening Post*, she also served as Director of Marketing for the Institute of Noetic Sciences. Founder and principal of The New Story, a coaching and consulting business focusing on helping people to discover deeper purpose in their lives, Oman Shannon lives with her husband in San Francisco. She can be reached at maggie@thenewstory.com.

TO OUR READERS

Conari Press publishes books on topics ranging from spirituality, personal growth, and relationships to women's issues, parenting, and social issues. Our mission is to publish quality books that will make a difference in people's lives—how we feel about ourselves and how we relate to one another. We value integrity, compassion, and receptivity, both in the books we publish and in the way we do business.

As a member of the community, we donate our damaged books to nonprofit organizations, dedicate a portion of our proceeds from certain books to charitable causes, and continually look for new ways to use natural resources as wisely as possible.

Our readers are our most important resource, and we value your input, suggestions, and ideas about what you would like to see published. Please feel free to contact us, to request our latest book catalog, or to be added to our mailing list.

2550 Ninth Street, Suite 101
Berkeley, California 94710-2551
800-685-9595 • 510-649-7175
fax: 510-649-7190 • e-mail: conari@conari.com
www.conari.com